ONE
TO
ONE

Self-Understanding
through
Journal Writing

ONE
TO
ONE

Self-Understanding through Journal Writing

CHRISTINA BALDWIN

M. Evans & Company, Inc.

Copyright © 1977, 1991 by Christina Baldwin

Library of Congress Cataloging-in-Publication Data

Baldwin, Christina

    One to one : self understanding through journal writing /
Christina Baldwin.
      p. cm.
    ISBN 0-87131-652-8 : $9.95
    1. Self-perception—Problems, exercises, etc. 2. Diaries—
Therapeutic use. 3. Diaries—Authorship. I. Title. II. Title: 1
to 1.
BF697.5.S43B34   1991
158′.1—dc20   91-4142
                                                   CIP

M. Evans and Company, Inc.
216 East 49 Street
New York, N.Y. 10017

Manufactured in the United States of America

9 8 7 6 5 4 3

Contents

Contents

ONE
TO
ONE
*Self-Understanding
through
Journal Writing*

Introduction: A Renaissance in Personal Writing

> When a person dies, a library is burned.
>
> —EDMUND WHITE

Journal writing has been around as long as writing itself. And before writing, people left their hand prints and paintings on cave walls, carved symbols into trees and cliffs, developed elaborate hieroglyphs, and kept oral tradition alive through memorization. When only a few could write, the village folk went to scribes and recited the letters they wanted sent or stories they wanted preserved. As writing became a more universal skill, people wanted to convey not only the commerce and business of life, but some kind of meaning, whatever was important to them about their individual story. All of us resonate, somewhere deep inside, with Edmund White's statement. "When a person dies, a library is burned." A unique experience of being human is lost.

All that we have learned about being human comes from what others have been willing to preserve of their accumulated knowledge and wisdom. So we understand our dependence, and we never know how great the loss of one life's story might be. It's not because we all need to write for the future, but because writing connects us to this chain of articulation about being human. Writing taps us in, like the sugar spike driven into the maple tree's trunk, to the veins of story and experience, some of which we claim as ours alone, and all of which are also universal.

As respect for individual life has risen over time, so, too, has respect for the individual story.

In a house thirty miles east of St. Paul, Minnesota, James Cummings, diarist and antiquarian book dealer, has the world's most complete, annotated collection of diaries and journals printed in or translated into English. In a large, wood-frame Victorian, which houses 80,000 books, Cummings maintains a collection of over 14,000 diaries and journals, which grows at the rate of several hundred a year. It takes over a thousand pages just to catalog and annotate the collection, and scholars come from around the country to study it.

Jim Cummings doesn't only collect diaries and journals, he keeps one: filling a page a day, every day. Since starting on his thirteenth birthday he hasn't missed a day or a line in over forty years. His great-grandmother started this tradition, and his children, now in their thirties, are the sixth generation keeping up this amazing family heritage.

In 1974, I went to the University of Minnesota community education program and asked if they knew about any courses in keeping a journal. I admitted, that I'd been keeping one myself for several years and, like so many of my students since, wasn't sure I was doing it right. They had never heard of such a course, and talked me into offering one. Jim Cummings and twelve Minneapolis and St. Paul poets showed up for that first class. We felt as though we were breaking ground, saying things for the first time, sharing thoughts we had had in private and had never spoken aloud. The whole idea of studying journal writing, seeing it as an art form and a life skill, was portentous; we knew it intuitively, but couldn't see the shape and scope of what was coming. It was winter, a time of long darkness in Minnesota. I remember us bundling up, leaving the attic of the little bookstore where we met, scuttling off into the night like conspirators, journals tucked in gloved hands. Same time next week. Same group.

In 1977, the first edition of *One to One* grew out of these early classes. I was thirty years old when I wrote it, and had the naive idea that the reason I was writing the book was to turn journal writing loose, to send my ideas off into the world. That much has been true. But I thought the ideas would just drift away, and I would have to figure out something else to do. I had no idea that an author and his or her work could become attached to each other, that I was creating a bond of responsibility between myself and readers of the book. Along with Morton Kelsey, writing about the spiritual journey, Ira Progoff, inventing the Intensive Journal®, and Tristine Rainer, combining various therapeutic techniques in the new diary, I rode the wave of interest in reflective writing. When *One to One* was first published, the Library of Congress had to create a new category for it: "1. diaries and journals, therapeutic uses of . . ."

These were pioneering times for journal writers. What has happened since is that our culture overall has chosen to value inner life much differently than we did a generation ago. Hundreds of thousands of people have decided that understanding what's happening to them internally is as important as knowing what is happening to them externally.

The journal has become such a phenomenon; it's even become a verb. "How often do you journal?" people ask me. Or they start a comment with, "I was journaling the other day . . ."

In this revised edition I have been able to update the original concepts, add sections, include new thoughts and expand entries. There's more life and perspective to add here because we have all grown from those first small circles of writers into a huge, private movement. Millions of blank books sell every year. More and more authors are writing about journal-keeping, and diaries and journals are now considered a valid literary genre. Every time I go to the bookstore or library I see how quickly this movement is growing. But what is visible is only the barest indication of what is really happening: for the essence of what is happening is that you are finding moments here and there and sitting down with a pen and blank paper. You are choosing to write and discovering the value in writing. You tap yourself in to the activity, to the history, to the legacy, to the promise. You learn as you go. You have made something come alive and become part of the culture that was not there twenty years ago. You should be proud of your interest, your commitment, your experimentation.

One to one, to one, to one, the writers write. Thank you.

Considerations for Blank Pages

WHAT IS A JOURNAL AND WHY KEEP ONE?

A journal is a book of dated entries. In a writing process that is beautifully adaptable to individual interests and preferences, dating the pages as we go may be the most unifying element of journal keeping. Each journal's contents are eclectic: reports of the day's events, recorded feelings, dreams, dialogues, fantasies, sketches, recipes, quotes from current reading material, cartoons and clippings, photographs and four-leaf clovers—whatever writers want to leave recorded in their passage through time. If you want to save something and be able to find it ten years from now, a journal makes a good place for tucking away the scraps of daily life. We discover this naturally by what we learn to put in writing, and by what we include in addition to writing.

My bookshelf of journals is over four feet long, an eclectic collection of differing styles, sizes, widths, formats. There are years of loose-leaf notebooks, bound in cardboard binders, and years of blank books—no longer blank, but filled with a tangible record of my life. This record is massively incomplete, yet tremendously important in its attempt to tell an authentic story *of* myself, *to* myself. Whenever I go through these volumes, as I did while writing this book, I am amazed at what I find there. Autumn leaves and pressed flowers, feathers, a photo of my grandmother and the two dozen roses we sent her for her ninetieth birthday, birth announcements and memorial cards, amateur drawings of my dreams—and words. Words beyond counting.

We will not ever get all of our lives down on paper. That is not the point of journal writing. Our lives are too complex, too quick-changing in thought and feeling. Things happen too fast. We live inside our lives aware of time-lapsed images of changing sky: clouds tumble and roil against the larger background, rains come, sometimes a cleansing wind, then clouds parting and sun again. Sitting at my desk, writing as quickly as I can, I am still only on the third paragraph and so much "weather" has occurred that it boggles my mind. What we leave in the journal is a code, a hint, the story of things which help us recall, on a very intimate level, the passage of those clouds, that day, the paths we took to arrive here in the middle of our lives. It is a very private conversation, which others may sometime read, but only we will every truly understand.

The words "diary" and "journal" are sometimes used interchangeably, but traditionally, diary connotes a more formal pattern of daily entries, serving primarily to record the writer's activities, experiences and observations. A diary tends to be outwardly focused. Diarist Thomas Mallon writes in the introduction of his book, *A Book of One's Own, People and their Diaries*, (Tichner & Fields, 1984):

> I try to write each night, but I often don't get around to writing up a day until several more have gone by. But I manage to keep them all separate. It's gone on this way for seven years now without any day missing its sentences. I suppose it's a compulsion, but I hesitate to call it that, because it's gotten pretty easy. . . . I can recall a few times when during the day I've decided not to do something (usually something small and mean) because I realized that if I did it I'd have to mention it to the diary that night.

In, *Our Private Lives*, (Vintage/Random House 1990) Author Gail Godwin, also an avid diarist, reports:

> . . . I discovered a fellow diarist over lunch and what a time we had discussing the intricacies of our venture-in-common, our avocation . . . specialty . . . compulsion? We confessed eccentricities. We examined our motives: why keep these records, year after year? What would happen if we stopped? Could we stop? We indulged in shoptalk: hardbound or softcover? lined or unlined? about how many pages a night? proportion of external events to internal?

Like Godwin and her lunching friend, you and I, as journal writers or aspiring journal writers, are about to engage in a session of shoptalk and writing suggestions.

However, in a commitment to journal writing for self-awareness, we are likely to write less about the world of external events and more about the world of internal reaction. We are writing our "weather," not *the* weather.

The word journal is loosely defined as an intermittent record of the inner life, written consistently, but not necessarily on a daily basis. A journal often provides a place for writers to explore the more subterranean aspects of themselves; those things which are the hardest to share with others, and often the hardest to understand even in our own minds. Mallon calls this pilgrimage writing and says:

> A breed apart from the diarists who write simply to collect the days or preserve impressions of foreign places are those who set out in their books to discover who they really are. These are generally very serious people, more in the way of pilgrims, with inward destinations, than mere travelers.

Well, I fit this profile and so, probably, do you. As people who take the journey of life seriously, we believe there are purposes to living which we need to discover, attend to, and fulfill. This doesn't mean that journal writing reflects only seriousness. Writing a journal provides relief during hard times and celebration during easy times. The exercises in this book will help you define and design your own writing agenda for the journal which you can undertake at your own pace. The questions posed here may be surprising, occasionally frightening, at least at first glance. They may generate an excited tumble of responses in your mind. As a tool for recording your inner and outer life, the journal will become as sophisticated or as simple as you make it—and there are times when you will want sophistication and there are times when you will want simplicity.

There are several assumptions implicit in journal writing for self-awareness.

The first assumption is that *we are capable of having a relationship with our own minds.* We are capable of building into our consciousness a point of observation of ourselves. This point of observation does not remove us from involvement with our lives, it serves an additional function, a special vantage point. To observe oneself from such a vantage point is not self-dividing; it acknowledges a many-sided self within the integration of a larger self. Observation makes it possible for one part of ourselves to write and another to read. Observation allows one part to ask and another to answer, one part to act and another to reflect, one part to explore and another to comprehend the exploration. *This duality is the experience of consciousness.*

As children, we are not usually conscious in this way, but we learn to be. From the time we are very small, grown-ups instruct us to "pay attention . . . look at what you're doing . . . think before you act . . . consider the consequences . . ." Out of all these instructions, consciousness finally springs. Not self-consciousness in the way that people feel suddenly shy when entering a room, but consciousness of ourselves as beings who are moving constantly through a web of interaction. We arrive at the beginning of wakefulness—aware that we are here, that a level of introspection is needed in order to continue.

Annie Dillard talks of this in her book, *An American Childhood* (Harper & Row, 1987). She discusses the coming of consciousness as an event of childhood, but it can happen at any age.

I woke in bits, like all children, piecemeal over the years. I discovered myself and the world, and forgot them, and discovered them again. I woke at intervals until, by that September when Father went down the river, the intervals of waking tipped the scales, and I was more often awake than not. I noticed this process of waking, and predicted with terrifying logic that one of these years not far away I would be awake continuously and never slip back, and never be free of myself again.

There are ways to get free of the self again, and eventually we reach them, though the journey through self-awareness is a long process of dedication to the self, treating ourselves and our consciousness like a garden we must water and weed and cultivate. In April 1970 I wrote about this in my journal, at the moment conscious awakening was occurring to me.

April 1970

I have been like Helen Keller, when she describes her early girlhood as "the Phantom," the little animal receiving dark sun and air, food and love, but unknowing what this sustenance was. Missing the vital comprehension, that infinitesimal link between thought and reality . . . until that flashing moment when she and Annie Sullivan stood beside the pump and Annie was spelling into Helen's hand, "w-a-t-e-r . . . w-a-t-e-r." And she KNEW! She understood and Annie shouted, "Captain, Mrs.

Keller . . . come quick . . . she knows!" Helen was spelling wildly, drinking well water and splashing, crazy with the joy of her comprehension. "w-a-t-e-r . . . w-a-t-e-r."

Even as I write this, the scene goes on now in my own breast—something new breaks open. I sit here drily, weeping for joy. My fingers, too, are spelling. This is my birth by the pump. This is my spring into consciousness.

The second assumption I make about this relationship with the mind is that *the relationship includes an available intelligence that is greater than we might think we have.* In the midst of thinking and writing about personal life issues, problems, themes, and patterns, we find ourselves in contact with a responding voice or presence or support. This greater intelligence is what we call insight, or intuition, or higher power. Everyone has it.

Journal writing opens up the labyrinth of our own thoughts until we find our way to this deeper intelligence. We are all accustomed to thinking on the surface: standing in the grocery store deciding between brands, handling detailed requests at work, navigating the complexities of busy lives. *Journal writing taps us into insight so that when we ask, we are answered.* When we act, we understand the motivations for acting. When we explore, we discover we do not live as only one unified consciousness of mind. There's a committee in the mind, and journal writing gives its members voices on the page. We hear the inner conversation, and are able to write it down so that we can observe and think about the ongoing debates which govern our internal lives and lead to our actions in the world.

July 1983

I feel like *all* the characters at the Mad Hatter's Tea Party. There are so many voices in my head, each with an opinion about what I should do regarding the book proposal. Each sure that its perspective is correct and the approach "we" should take.

"Go for it, you can do it."

"I don't want to do it. The idea isn't interesting enough to me."

"That's immaterial, you have to earn a living . . ."

"I'll resist you the whole time if you . . ." Etcetera, etcetera.

I read somewhere years ago a quote from Mark Twain, who said, "The only person who can use the word 'we' when referring to himself is the King of England and a man with tapeworms." Well, I hate to mention it, but he was wrong: everybody seems to be a "we."

The third, and most comforting assumption is that *these mental exchanges of dialogue and decision-making are benevolent.* The mind consistently tries to make the best decision it can for us, and with us. The mind is constantly searching out—according to its understanding at the moment—the best options for our health, growth, survival. To an outsider, our decision-making process may sometimes look bizarre. Even to ourselves, looking back on past choices from the vantage point we have now, it may be hard to believe that we were attempting to find "the best option." However, the more we probe our lives for self-understanding, the more we begin to see this is so.

Listening to a friend tell the story of his alcoholism, it made sense that in his large, exuberant family, drinking was linked to security and belonging. When he began to join the adults in beer drinking at age sixteen, he felt initiated into a loving community.

"Of course, you became an alcoholic," I responded. "Drinking was all wrapped up in how your family defined who belonged." A woman who, throughout her childhood, was told that she was just like her brother, discovered that her years of making choices just to finally be defined as a separate person by the family kept her as bound to this prediction as if she had followed directly in his footsteps. Eventually, she set out in the journal to define and find herself. Other people's stories remind me to look again at the patterns in my own family, to discern which beliefs and behaviors, which no longer help me function well in the world, once helped me function very well in my historical family.

August 1979

How I decide something:

1. I come up with an idea and get really excited.

2. I tell a few friends and develop my story of what I intend to do.

3. My brain kicks in and I find out what everyone in my head thinks I should do. Most of their suggestions are in conflict with the rest of their suggestions.

4. I get depressed. Decide I can't get what I want.

5. I get angry. Decide to defy the lot of them.

6. I use the anger to wrest permission to do what I intended anyway. I look pretty silly sometimes

13

being so mad, when no one externally is putting up a fight.

I don't like this pattern. I want to be able to make decisions without going through such a long internal loop. How am I going to learn this? What part of myself can I use as the one who is in charge?

Many messages have been fed into each individual's psyche: messages which have shaped self-esteem, expectations of success and failure, psychological limitations and permissions. These assumptions show up in journal writing page after page. Our assumptions may remain invisible to us for a long time because they are deeply integrated into our self-view and our world-view. This inability to see our beliefs directly is natural—yet so is our ability to steadfastly discover what these beliefs are and how they drive our lives. As we become aware, we can decide whether or not we want a certain belief to continue driving us, and what new or modified beliefs will allow us to have the kind of life we desire. This examination is the essence of introspective writing.

In the journal, our assumptions may remain hidden in the syntax of our language, a code beneath the obvious meaning of the sentences, a signal to ourselves from these understood, unconscious beliefs. Eventually we will write something obvious, such as: "*I wish I could* ____ *but I'm* ____." Perhaps this sentence reads, "*I wish I could go back to school, but I'm not smart enough.*" Over and over again the writer prefaces thinking about school with this limiting assumption. She doesn't consciously "read" it, it's just there in her writing, part of the webbing of her thought, a statement of fact. Then, one day, looking through her journals, the sentence pops out at her and she questions it. Once she begins to question, she can experience everything we have been talking about: consciousness, insight, and the willingness of the mind to make a new decision based on better information.

Life is a process of trial and error. Eventually, we will reach our insights, but writing a journal speeds up the process and gives us a structured way to review our beliefs and change our minds. This was the original meaning of the word "therapy," to attend to our mental functions. To watch them, interact with them, change them, and lead them in the directions we need our lives to grow. *Therapy is whatever is applied to a situation or condition that brings about healing.*

In early Greek, *therapeutikφs* meant to attend to, and a *therápōn* was the attendant, or midwife, who made way for Psyche's head. In this fuller definition, therapy means to stretch one's limbs, or consciousness, opening oneself to the imagery and activity of labor. Therapy means to give birth to, as well as to heal. This joining of meanings—to heal and to birth—is what journal writing for self-awareness offers us. We attend to our own lives. We learn to heal. We labor and give birth to the selves we are intended to be.

This is a task for both women and men, an invitation to consciousness. In the relationship within our minds, we attend to our labors. What we write in the journal is the record of this relationship made tangible.

April 1981
I made it! I realize finally that there's nothing wrong with me. No fatal flaw. I'm okay. I don't have to defend against the secret belief that I'm not okay, that I shouldn't be here, because I don't believe it anymore.

Therapy is a wonderful gift sometimes, especially when the message gets through to the darkest corners of myself. I can be alive!

In the car, yesterday and today, I burst into shouts of triumph, interspersed with tears of grief. It took me thirty-five years from the first cry to this one. If the baby is alive inside me, we can go on as one person.

The more we ask of ourselves in the writing process, the more inner labor will occur. As in any relationship, the more we are listened to and responded to, the more we discover what we can share.

We are having this relationship with the self anyway, even if we're not yet conscious of it. Journal writing is the practice of admitting *therapeutikφs*, admitting that we do attend to inner life. In journal writing classes, people worry about the level at which they are writing—that they can't get deeper into this conversation, or sometimes that they can't seem to come up for air and notice the day around them. There is an inherent balance in the mind, a gyroscope. The mind takes care of itself. It takes care of you. Your written conversations will rise and fall as you are ready to pay attention to different things. Your role is to interact, respond, initiate, think about, and go on. Every day you create more life, and when you have time and interest and energy—you write it down.

WHAT THIS BOOK IS ABOUT

The main section of this book, Journal Writing for Self-Awareness, is a series of topics which illuminate various aspects of inner life. The topics are chosen for the purpose of expanding and deepening choices for writing. Though the subjects are presented separately, in the reality of journal writing they tend to mingle together naturally. Our minds are associative. We are living examples of random access memory: One thought leads to another thought, and another, in a unique and individual pattern.

If I put an object in the middle of a table where a group of journal writers are sitting and say, "Start here, with this apple—or rose, or book, or even a common thought—and write for five minutes," every writer will make his or her own unique associations. Every writer will arrive at his or her unique destination. This is the way our minds work, and the topics in the book are separated only for illustrative purposes.

Throughout the text, I have included quotes from published materials and entries from my own private writings. In this manner I hope to illustrate both the community of writing in which we all participate and allow you to glimpse details from one particular journey. It is not particularly important that this journey is mine. I have used it because mine is the only journey I have access to.

I have been teaching journal writing since 1975 and have worked with tens of thousands of people, spent hours in rooms full of writers, silent but for the scratching of pens, the electronic tapping of a laptop computer, the quiet buzz of someone reciting into a tape recorder, the steady poke, poke, poke of a braille writer, and I have never seen another person's journal. We may read aloud to each other a few minutes, share an entry here and there, but journal writing is a private activity. Journal writing is a sacred contract with our own privacy. I would not ask anyone, in the middle of his or her writing journey, to turn it over to me for sampling . . . so the only samples I have are my own.

I trust the ability of these samples to communicate because I trust that the intimate describes the whole. Though the circumstances of our lives may differ greatly, we are all involved in similar life-struggles and a similar search for relationship and healing within the mind. May the ways I have recorded and reflected upon the experiences in my life help you translate your own experiences to into writing. Do not do it "my" way—*use these samples and exercises to develop a way of your own.*

Journal writing is a voyage to the interior. This voyage contains the same elements as our lives, thoughts, and feelings. The journals will be brilliant and boring; they will be superficial and profound; they will be humorous and hazardous. If we are in a state of open exploration and self-acceptance with our lives in general, it will become apparent in our journal writing. If we are closed down, frightened, confused, that, too, will be apparent in writing. There are times in our lives when we temporarily lose confidence and perspective. The journal will not prevent such occurrences, but it will make a difference in the extent of the loss and it will shorten the length of time we spend being lost. The act of journal writing increases our capacity to track down what is happening, and put ourselves back on track. When there is a problem with which we need outside perspective or protection, insights in the journal may be carried into counseling, treatment, Twelve Step groups, spiritual direction, and other forms of therapeutic assistance.

The honest appraisal inherent in the journal relationship declares our readiness to assume responsibility for our growth and to assert our power to deal with our lives. Responsibility is a key word in journal writing and often a frightening or confusing concept. We use the word without having a personal definition of it, and most of us come out of backgrounds where taking responsibility was not rewarded. "Who's responsible for this?!" was a clarion call to punishment. Stepping forward, trembling, trying to be brave, to face teachers and parents and the old man next door, confessing to priests or wrestling directly with our consciences, were confusing situations in which responsibility became linked with anger, shame, penalty, and humiliation. We ended up believing that to "accept responsibility" was to foolishly scapegoat ourselves while others continued to get away with the same behavior. We may have continued to try to be responsible, but our beliefs grew more and more conflicted. Yet journal writing for self-awareness leads us directly to the issue of responsibility.

This book is about our ability to redefine, reaccept and reempower ourselves by learning to take appropriate responsibility. To be responsible, according to the dictionary, is to be accountable for something "within one's power to control or manage." You are not responsible for the weather, not even if you're a weather forecaster. You *are* responsible for driving safely through a blizzard, for keeping away from trees in a lightning storm, for getting your family into the basement when the tornado siren blows.

If you accept the challenge of learning responsibility, your first commitment must be to create a flexible, changing, updatable idea of what is in your power to control or manage. In some cases, insight will lead you to increase the sense of what's under your control, and in other cases insight will lead you to shrink the area of control, or change your assumptions about it. A friend of mine who is a Presbyterian minister has developed a morning invocation ritual for herself. One of the lines in her personal prayer for the day is, "Help me be true to myself—and true to the universe. Keep me from over-responsibility—and irresponsibility." We are always working on where the line is drawn, and coming to new awareness about responsibility that frees us to lead fuller lives.

As we explore responsibility in the journal, and understand it better in our lives, responsibility becomes a declaration of power. *If we are responsible for something, we empower ourselves with the ability to change it.* To make effective changes, we must have appropriate boundaries around responsibility and the willingness to change our minds over and over without embarrassment. This is updating: Once I believed this . . . now I believe this. As we become more practiced journal writers, much of this vacillation can occur in the privacy of the journal first; then we can experiment with changing behaviors which other people see.

When I was a child, I developed exaggerated beliefs about what I was responsible for in my family. I tried to maintain calm, to hold my parents' relationship together, to help raise the younger children. I did not really have such responsibilities, or wield such power in the family. It was a fantasy.

In my early thirties, I spent years using the journal to become aware of these beliefs, noticing the detrimental impact they were having on my life, and then replacing them with new beliefs. This was not a calm process. My life felt internally chaotic. I ranted and railed and complained on the page. I defended one belief or another valiantly, only to realize six months later that I had to give it up. I learned to ask very specific questions, such as:

- How does this belief affect me today?

- Is this a positive influence?

- What other belief could I replace this with?

- What would have to change in order for my belief to change?

- If this belief is linked to my sense of security, what different kind of security will I need to develop?

- How will my willingness to change my mind benefit me?

August 1984

I am changing my mind, and my whole life feels changed. I've decided to stop worrying about getting cheated in all these current business deals and to switch from a mental framework of "lack" to an expectation of generosity.

There's a Zen saying that the mind is a drunken monkey, meaning that it's scattered and undisciplined. I've been feeling that a lot lately. I light sage and pray, but I don't get still. I don't understand the difference between giving up and giving in and my mind is panicky. I drive myself, literally, to distraction. And so finally, I get ready to change my mind: to calm down; to look for the orderliness of all the decisions I have to make instead of looking at their disorder. What is the difference here, are there different rooms in my mind? One of them full of chaos? One of them able to see the way through?

This book is full of questions, and your journals need to be full of questions, too. Questioning is how we lead ourselves into new awareness. We write in response to questions, whether or not the questioning is openly addressed on the page, or even conscious. The more specific the question, the more specific the response. Consider the following snatches of dialogue:

"Hi, how are yah?"
"Fine. And you?"

or:

"You're looking chipper today. What's the secret?"
"I'm getting married next month, and I got pro-moted at work. I haven't been this happy in years. Feels like things are finally coming together for me."

How we ask questions, what questions we ask, and how we respond to them determine the insights we have and the rate at which we will grow. This book is full of questions. They are questions designed to teach the art of questioning. Not every question will fit for you, but one or another may trigger your own thoughts so that you come up with exactly the right question that you need to address next in your journal.

January 1991

TWENTY QUESTIONS FOR THE NEW YEAR:

1. How's the new book going to do?

2. Is there something I should be doing to help it that I'm not?

3. What's the next thing I need to explore, for my own career growth, my life purpose, my next project?

4. How will I create the time and energy to work on the FL material?

5. How will I find time to write in my journal and meditate, take care of the new puppy, plan regular exercise, and still be ready to work by 9:00 AM?

6. What am I not reflecting on that I need to?

7. What am I learning working for XYZ?

8. How is E's health?

9. Will my grandma live to celebrate her one hundredth birthday next fall?

10. How do we hang on to the best that we have while letting ourselves grow? ... etcetera.

Questioning is an adventure available to everyone. Questioning is a form of power which allows us to restructure our lives from the page outward. Questioning and responsibility are deeply linked, because responsibility is often what we need to question first. Though I considered myself an overly responsible child, there were also many ways in which I misunderstood and avoided true responsibilities—not only in childhood, but for years after—because I was so busy trying to carry out my fantasy responsibilities, and there was no one clear enough to teach me what true responsibility might be. The journal has taught me. There is something magic about a pen and paper when it is combined with the willingness to question and the determination to break free and discover one's own true self and the life one is meant to lead.

As a teacher, I am asked unusual questions from time to time. Not long ago, someone asked me what I thought the most important decision was that I'd ever made. My answer was quick and spontaneous—the decision to keep a journal. Because keeping a journal, the way I keep a journal, has led to every other important decision I've made, and led to the unmaking of many decisions which no longer serve me well. I hope that keeping a journal will be as rich, challenging, and playful an adventure also for you.

VOICES IN THE CULTURE

Society has changed significantly in the last third of the twentieth century. Three kinds of change affect us directly as journal writers: changes in our expectations about what sort of human beings we should be; changes in our expectations about the quality of life we ought to be able to create; and changes in our experience of the power of the individual within the power of the group.

These expectations are fairly universal, though the discussion of what they mean changes by culture and by subgroup. A high-finance deal maker and an Amish farmer have very different definitions of these expectations, but these elements are deeply at work in both their lives. If we look closely at the world, we see that much of the turmoil, both on the scale of individual life-change and the grand scale of governmental systems, is driven by changing expectations about what life is supposed to provide.

As journal writers setting out to define our relationship to the whole of life, we are confronted with the forces of the prevailing culture. We are not writing in a vacuum. When I get up in the morning, I stumble into the kitchen, turn on the teapot, and glance at the newspaper before I head back to my desk and time for journal writing. I keep trying to break myself of this habit, wishing I would go first to the journal and then to the usually gruesome details of the latest news story and a few minutes of chuckles of the comics, but I don't seem to be willing to change my routine. And maybe that's all right, because I am not separated from the news, I am living within its influence. The impact is there, whether I write first or read first. And the realities of the world have their place in my journal and their acknowledgement in my journey. These realities deserve our attention, and outrage, our compassion and concern.

May 1990

Driving across town to teach, I heard a radio piece on the children of Mozambique who have been victims of a four-year civil war. The narrator, skilled at evoking the necessary mental picture to accompany audio journalism, tells of being present at the interview of a small boy who was kidnapped by the rebels, forced to become a soldier, and brainwashed and emotionally bound to his unit. Julius is his name. He says he is fourteen, though the reporter says he is small, innocent looking, the size of a ten-year-old. I hear the halting voice of this child, reciting without emotion the atrocities that have been done to him.

The head of the Save the Children Foundation is interviewed. He says they need more money to help bring these children back to the sunny, dusty villages and reintegrate them into their families and social groups. The most successful healing process they've discovered is to reintroduce these children to their home communities and allow them to tell their stories. To dance out their experiences, to have the focus of the campfire. . . .

Someone takes them home. Someone says, "Here is Julius. He has been stolen away and now he is returned. He has been forced to do terrible things, to kill people in cold blood. He is your son, your brother, your clansman . . . forgive him . . . welcome him." And they do. These children are being saved by communities which still practice forgiveness.

Why doesn't forgiveness work in America? Is the difference in the children and their ability to recover? Or in the communities and their abilities to absorb and reintegrate those who have been stolen from them? I think about the boys who went "wilding" and nearly killed that young woman in Central Park, and it makes me more afraid for what is missing in my own culture than for what is happening in Mozambique.

Journal writing is a tool arising out of introspection. The journal illuminates the self. And the individual self illuminates the collective self. As we heal the self we begin to heal the whole. The things I discover and commit to as important values for myself become the values I want to see reflected in my community, my country, and my planet. And I know that I cannot fully have these values unless I work to see that this emerging quality of life is indeed available for my community, my country, and my planet.

Instead of saying "Amen," the Native Americans of the prairie tribes end their prayers by saying "All my relatives." Relatives include everything made of earth, air, fire and water. They have an understanding of their connectedness to life and their responsibility, which they consider to be a wide hoop, inside which all life must be drawn in and considered. So must it be in the journal and in our destinations.

Poet Robert Graves said, "There is one story only." You and I and all our relatives are the story. Our lives move through the story. In the journal, as we come to understand our personal stories, we develop an intuitive intelligence about the nature of human beings that may be translated from the self to the world. We become articulate voices in the midst of change, capable of working from within the dynamic and not against it.

The intelligence that emerges in journal writing is not limited to people of any particular background or education. The voice of the journal writer is the voice of struggle with life's intimate challenges. The voice carries a validity that transcends race, gender, age, religion, or income. These attributes, so long regarded as appropriate divisions between people, become only the fabric of diversity in which our common struggles are recorded.

Writing Basics for the Journal

CREATING YOUR OWN JOURNAL STYLE

There is a little of the fetishist in each of us, and it often emerges while devising the "perfect" arrangement for journal-keeping. Arrangements I have seen include three-ring notebooks of varying sizes and decoration, sketch pads, various forms of art and business-supply materials, ledgers and stenography pads, bound blank books, and assorted spiral notebooks. I have seen people use laptops and personal computers. One friend has half of a hard disk full of journal entries, none of them printed out on paper; she accesses them by dates and codes when she wants to review something. Many bookstores now have a carousel of blank books, and there is a shop across town which imports exquisite blank books and accompanies this selection with fine pens. Shops like these exist in many towns and cities, and they have grown in direct response to the numbers of people writing journals. Ten million blank books sell each year. And in the middle of the era of "the rolling-ball-fine-point-felt-tip-marker," there has been resurgence of the use of fountain pens. The dark, mysterious smell of ink is wafting again to the nostrils of private writers.

This attention to the physical details of journals and journal writing may sound facetious, but it is meant in earnest. In journal writing we allow ourselves to venture deep into the writing process, and the kind of notebook, paper, and writing instrument we use will either foster or hinder our progress. We experience a pleasure that is part of journal keeping when we create a form uniquely our own. Beginning a journal or starting a new volume is an excuse to indulge yourself a little. It may take you months to fill a book. How nice the associations can be, thinking back to a day in a season now past, when you took a little time to go wandering in and out of stationers, hefting the weight of blank books in your hands, holding a pen, choosing a new ink color—or several colors— deciding that the card a friend just sent you is perfect for the cover. This is not about getting fancy or expensive; it's about creating a pleasurable link to the object you're writing in.

There are many ways to express creativity in the journal. I am constantly delighted with the very particular styles people have developed. One man I know writes his journal in a code he developed himself. And a woman acquaintance writes a journal consisting only of letters, to both real and imaginary characters in her life. Another divides her pages into two columns—objective, and subjective—and writes simultaneous ledgers of what she thinks is happening and how she feels about what is happening. Some people write with a tumbling-out style that doesn't differentiate between real and imaginary dialogues, dreams and daily occurrences, the relationships one is really having with people versus relationships one would like to have with people. As long as you are writing for yourself, you don't have to meet anyone else's standards but your own. And your own interests, standards, and format will change over time. Journal writing is an evolving experiment.

THE WRITING PROCESS

There are several basic techniques which facilitate journal writing. They form the basis of much that will be introduced later. They are simple, and will ease your entry and re-entry into writing.

FLOW WRITING

Flow writing is the most basic form of writing in the journal. It "flows" back and forth between the writing and responding mind. You don't need to know what you're going to say before you sit down and start writing. Flow writing allows you to follow your stream of consciousness and put it in words on the page. It's simple and quick.

To begin flow writing, prepare to write, and then look around your environment—choose anything that strikes your eye and use it as the opening image, your starting point. Then allow yourself to free associate to whatever this image calls to mind. Keep free associating. At the beginning, it's helpful to limit the time of flow writing. Set a timer for five, six, or seven minutes and see what happens to your train of thought.

The example below was written in six minutes while I was leading a journal seminar.

January 1990

This church basement has my grandpa's paintings on the wall. Not really, of course, but heavy oils that look like the landscapes that used to hang over the couch and fireplace in my childhood homes. He lived nearby and used to come to Sunday dinner and stand thoughtfully in front of last year's mountain land-scapes, as though admiring some artist other than himself. I've not thought of him in a long time, a man who seems to have had little impact on me, and dis-appeared into fifteen years of senility which my mother took care of by carting him off with her to Canada because he needed family nearby.

I remember his three surviving children bringing his ashes back to Minneapolis to be buried in the cem-etery next to his second wife's grave. His first wife, my grandmother, is not dead yet. Is hanging onto each advancing year of her nineties. I sometimes wonder if she really wants to be alive or if living is simply a habit she can't give up. Maybe she's afraid to give it up. I hope not. I hope her dream of the universe is gentle.

That's all we've really got to go on, our particular dreams of reality. The dream of the universe we carry inside ourselves determines how we see the world, what we imagine of both life and death. Belief frames everything. I understand this more and more at this time in my life when external circumstances stay fairly stable, and my internal circumstances vacillate wildly. Depression—despair—optimism—faith: all are states determined in my mind. I am trying to fig-ure out how to have more control over my own thought process. I don't like being at the mercy of my mind and keep looking for a key that might open myself to deeper serenity.

Serenity is a word I never used to hear, and I'm still not sure/

The slash-mark is the point where the buzzer rang, and the group and I stopped writing. It's frustrating to stop in the middle of a thought, but it has a good purpose, too. *Writing comes out of tension, out of the need to say something.* The act of interrupting yourself, during a week of timed flow-writing, in which you stop each time the buzzer rings, will create a healthy tension. Soon you will long to write more. Your mind will organize its thoughts before you put them down. Your confidence will grow until you don't feel that writing ten, fifteen, or twenty minutes is scary. Disciplining yourself with timed entries is a good way to prime your journal-writing pump whenever you have run dry, or fallen away from the practice for awhile.

Ignoring your journal is a natural part of journal writing. It happens when for one reason or another writing is temporarily not as important as it was. When this happens to you, simply start again by reestablishing your relationship to the journal through flow writing.

Since the above example is my own, I can analyze it a little to illustrate how flow writing tends to work in the journal. First there is the chosen image (the painting) which often leads to a bit of reminiscence about why this thing caught one's eye (Grandpa on Sunday afternoons). After this, the free association begins to work more quickly (burial, to Grandmother, to my own questions about the universe). In free association, writing spontaneously begins to deepen. What is currently on my mind, at a level I may not have stopped to articulate, comes to the surface and finds its way easily into sentences. Now that I have reached a real thought, I could write for a long time about the topic which has emerged. In fact, after this flow-writing exercise, the topic of serenity keeps emerging in the journal for several weeks, even though I was propelled back into a busy work project and had very little reflective time. When I did make my way to the journal, the quest for serenity was always there.

People often decide to keep journals as the result of one of two situations. One is a sudden decision that it's time to organize our thoughts, or bundle together all those scraps of paper where we've been jotting little notes to ourselves. Another is a crisis. We are going through a major disruption or change and it's creating large amounts of stress. The need to dump our confusion outside our minds where we can take a look at it, and to clear enough space in the inner conversation for new dialogue to occur leads to the sense that we will write—or burst. In either situation, flow writing provides a way to settle into the habit of writing and find the connection that will carry us through so much of the work of the journal.

Whatever situation you find yourself in, try setting aside whatever time feels comfortable to you for several weeks, and collect a stack of flow writing entries. It's probably not important that you even read these—just keep going. When you're ready to review, go back through them and underline the recurring themes that you see building within them. These topics are an informal agenda. They reveal what's really on your mind.

Years ago, teaching journal writing in a nursing home, I sent the class off to flow write for a week and one woman came back with a dozen entries, all of which talked about her mother. This woman was, herself, nearly eighty and her mother had been dead for many years.

However, it was obvious that the relationship between them was unfinished, so I taught her the next technique and she was able to resolve her relationship through writing about it.

DIALOGUE WRITING

All journal writing is a result of the ongoing conversation we are having in the mind, the slipstream of thought. In the act of writing, we are in dialogue; our words only appear on the page as monologue. For many of the upcoming journal exercises, it will be useful to allow this dialogue to emerge directly on the page and master the art of asking questions. Through question and answer you can help direct your thoughts. Dialogue taps us into the greater intelligence of our minds. We break through our defenses and confusion to our intuitive understanding of what's going on.

To start dialoguing on the page, ask an opening question and assign that voice a name or symbol. Take a breath. Start the next line by writing down the response that occurs to the question and assign the responding voice a name or symbol. Write down the first response that comes to the surface of your thoughts, even if you don't think it makes sense. Allow yourself to be led by these exchanges, to become part of the wondering process. Don't try to predetermine the outcome.

Dialoguing is an exercise in learning to hear and trust our inner voices. You can use pens with two colors of ink. You can draw a line down the middle of the page and have one voice write on the left side, one voice write on the right. If you don't have an idea "who" is talking, use numbers or letters. X and O are frequent voices in my journal. It doesn't matter if I name them. The dialogues work just as effectively without my bothering to pinpoint the exact identity of my mind's many voices.

You can dialogue with anything. All you do is divide the monologue voice of the journal into two voices which respond to each other. The same day I wrote about my grandfather, I realized that my upper back was knotted with tension. It was physically uncomfortable, so when I taught the group dialoguing techniques, I wrote the following dialogue with my shoulder blades.

January 1990

ME:　　What's going on with you this morning? The rest of my body seems pretty calm, but you are sure tense.

BACK: No I won't and you can't make me. No I won't and you can't make me.

ME:　　What does that mean?

BACK: It's my stubbornness chant.

ME:　　I hear that. What are you being stubborn about?

BACK: I don't know. I could run a list of thoughts, but I think it's just verbiage to give you since you asked, not the real issue.

ME:　　When I close my eyes, I see a picture of a baby, very tense in her mother's arms. She is too little to get away, but she doesn't want to be held.

BACK: I remember feeling like that. It was a long time ago.

ME:　　Yes. What has then got to do with now?

BACK: The resistance to trust is tied up in these muscles. You want to be serene and the baby is not serene. A baby has to trust, but what if the caregiver is not trustworthy? There is no choice. If the baby decides not to trust, she destroys something in her psyche. If I had decided that, you'd be pretty crazy. But it was very confusing to have to decide over and over again to trust untrustworthiness. I did the best I could, but trusting makes me very tense.

ME: I know you did the best you could. I believe you. *Do you believe you?*

BACK: Yes.

ME: *So, what has now got to do with then?*

BACK: Now, even though we are grown-up, we are placed in the same position: we have to trust because a lot of the changes we are making we cannot control. I am afraid that some of the key people I am being asked to trust right now are not trustworthy.

ME: That is one way to see the situation, and it makes sense. But the outcome hasn't occurred yet, so you don't know whether this situation is really like the old one or not. And besides, I know a lot more now than I did then. And I am capable of taking care of myself. We don't have to be dependent in that old way.

BACK: *But you still have to trust?*

ME: Yes, I do. I am not blindly trusting those people you are worried about, I am trusting the process. I am trusting our life. I am trusting God. And by the way, your old mom wasn't in charge of that baby either—God was in charge of that baby. *Now, how is your stubbornness?*

BACK: I'm trying to sort it out so I can see life differently.

ME: *What if you imagine angel hands holding your back, supporting you?*

BACK: Feels good. *But do I still have to trust __?*
ME: NO! But it will help if you trust the process.
BACK: Okay, I get it.
ME: *Will you relax now?*
BACK: Yes.
ME: I know there's more to think about all this. We can continue talking later if you like.
BACK: Yes, but I understand this piece. Watch me relax.

Dialogue writing is amazingly easy for most people, even though before you try it you may not be able to imagine how to do it. In every class, there are usually a few people staring at me with anxiety, perplexed about the process and sure it's not going to work for them. Once we are settled into the actual writing, I notice they are working easily and quickly, switching voices line by line.

The purpose of dialogue is insight: to get at material which is buried beneath the layer of monologue. I could have written a little essay to myself about the tension in my shoulders and not uncovered any of the information that came quickly to the surface in this dialogue. I could have written about tension off and on for months, earnestly looking at the problem, but avoiding the direct questions which unlock the key.

The questions are printed here in italics. Notice how the specificity that we were talking about earlier, works in written dialogue: the more specific the question, the more specific the response. When you write in dialogue, it's much easier to get to the heart of an issue than when you write in monologue. When I break into dialogue in the journal, I know I'm ready to deal with whatever's been on my mind.

The insights that come from dialogue don't always have to be serious. Dialogue is a way of having fun, too.

August 1990

CB: Hello, sunshine. Hello, lake. I can hardly believe I'm here, it's so beautiful.

Day: You're welcome in this day. You can be the day's daughter, all day long. If I could grant you one wish, what would it be?

CB: Ohh, that's easy—to be fully present. To feel the warmth of the sun, to hear the lapping of the waves, to not use my mind to wander into the past or the future, but to just be here, now, on this rock, writing . . . doodling, maybe.

Day: Doodling would be nice. Can you draw sailboats?

After I gave a speech recently, a former student came up to me with a big smile on her face. "I just want to tell you something you already know," she said. "Dialoguing has changed the whole pattern of my journal writing. In fact, it's probably the basis for most of the changes I've made in the past five years. I just talk to myself until I'm clear and ready to move. I had no idea you were giving me such a powerful tool."

She's right, I do know the power of dialogue, and the reason I know it is because I use dialogue more and more myself.

PROTECTING YOUR PRIVACY

The most valuable thing about a journal is that it's a tangible record of your life. You can hold it in your hands and carry it around with you. You can read and reread it. This tangibility is both the most satisfying *and* the most vulnerable aspect of your journal because someone else can hold it and carry it around and read it, too. The need for privacy, to write what we want without censoring ourselves with fear of exposure or disapproval, is an issue for every journal writer.

In a class for new journal writers, we were only half an hour into the course and had done one flow writing exercise when a woman at the back raised her hand and asked, "What do I do with this when I die?" The students laughed—but nervously—because it was a question occurring in their minds, too. "How am I going to take care of this thing?" is a question that arises almost immediately. It is a serious question, not a laughing matter, for we *will only write to the level of our protection.* If you are afraid that your spouse or partner or children or parents will violate your privacy and read the journal; *if you are afraid* that you might get run over by a truck and the family will read your journals, even though you've told them you want them burned, *you will censor yourself.* You won't be honest in the ways you write about the people you are afraid will read what you have written. If you fear intrusion into this delicate process, you won't be honest about the more difficult things you need to say about yourself, to admit from your experience, and to attempt to make peace with.

- What kind of privacy do you need in order to write about topics which are most important and scary to you?

- How are you going to create that privacy?

Privacy and the protection of your journal is a complex issue. *Respecting your privacy is a commitment to take care of the journal as a physical object* so that you may confront the other hindrances to writing honestly. If you inhibit your writing by not taking appropriate care of your journals, then you never get to discover and break through the other inhibitors to find your real voice.

Anais Nin, whose major life work was a journal she kept from age eleven to her seventies, stored her journals in a bank vault. Beatrix Potter, who lived with strict Victorian parents while she wrote children's tales, created a code when she was nine that took years for the executors of her estate to decipher. Students have shared a number of interesting ways they take care of their journals: hiding them in the cookbooks because they are sure no one else in the family looks there, locking them in a desk drawer, locking them in a briefcase in the car's trunk; or very directly showing the journal to the family and raising the issue of privacy and respect, buying a journal for everyone and saying "if you're curious, do this yourself." Here are some issues to consider:

- How are you going to take care of your journals, the one you are writing now, and the ones that you have already written?

- What fantasies of outside readership inhibit your writing?

- If you were absolutely guaranteed of your privacy, what inhibitions would remain?

- What do you think you want done with your journals when you die?

- Who can you talk to about these wishes and trust to carry them out?

- Where will you keep your written instructions for dispersal of the journals? (And keep these instructions updated, if you change your mind.)

We have all developed a sense of our need for privacy through the respect or violation of it in the past and through our experiences in trusting others and being trusted by others. We have been angered at violations of our own privacy, and have violated other people's privacy. As a teenager, I drilled a hole in my diary notebook and padlocked it with my combination gym-lock. I hid it in my closet, in the basement, under the bed, moving it from place to place in ritualistic evasive actions. To further protect myself, I wrote the most secret parts of an entry in the middle of the page where it couldn't be read, even if pried open from above or below. My fierce protectiveness stemmed from feeling that most of the things I wrote were not settled in myself. Testing my emotions, exploring romantic and sexual feelings, revealing dreams for myself as a woman, were all too fragile to withstand scrutiny or judgement. I feared that what was most precious to me would be considered cute or immature by adults.

September 1960

Tonight on the school bus, I thought to myself: well, home to hell. Isn't that terrible? Yet it's the way I feel. Mom complains that I don't do any work or help her, but she doesn't see that I don't like to be around her. She keeps hounding me. Silence is golden. Oh, what truth in the phrase. I have showed no outward sign of the way I feel, but she has sensed it. We can't be close in any way. It almost seems as if we were never mother and daughter, for we are only stranger and stranger.

She takes this out on me by not letting me watch the television programs I want: Sunday, no "Little Women" or "National Velvet," Thursday, no "The United Nations Reports."

Even though I was acutely aware of my own need for privacy, this did not prevent me from going through my mother's closets from time to time. I uncovered some of her private papers. I looked through the Playboy under my brother's mattress. We are paranoid about privacy, because we know that we have impulses to invade the privacy of others. And we know we have followed these impulses from time to time, even against our better judgement or proclaimed values.

Privacy is an emotional issue. Protecting the journal raises a number of questions which may not seem related to journal keeping at all:

- What are your feelings about privacy and sharing in general?

- What ways have you taken care of your privacy that you feel good about?

- What ways have you ignored your need for privacy and later felt bad about?

- How has your privacy been invaded, and do you still need to make peace with these experiences?

- What ways have you disregarded the privacy of others, and do you still need to make amends?

- How do you communicate your needs for privacy?

- How do you communicate the importance of your journal's privacy to those you live with?

- Do you grant them equal privacy?

One way to deal with privacy is to encourage journal writing among family or household members. When several people in a group keep journals, everyone's perspective changes. It becomes obvious that, while other people are included in the journal, the purpose of the writing is to sort out our own minds. Journal writing is a healthy form of self-centered activity. I may be writing about you, but I'm really thinking about myself, my relationship to you, a problem, a memory, or a goal. Anyone who keeps a journal very long becomes aware of the essential self-centeredness of journal writing and less curious about what someone else is writing. It's also a good general maxim that journal keeping facilitates communication, and unless what you are writing about is the irrevocable breakdown in a relationship, chances are that keeping a journal will help build a stronger, more empathetic bond between partners, within families, or among friends.

Both my partner and I keep journals, and knowing that these pages are safe in the same house, that the privacy around these pages is mutually protected, we are free to read *to* each other from time to time, to help each other with problem solving, to witness each other's process of growth and insight. But even when you have created a circle of privacy and safety that feels comfortable at home, incidents of intrusion may occur.

Several years ago, in the middle of teaching a seminar, my journal disappeared for twenty-four hours. I had set it down to move to the front of the room and begin the next class session; when I went back to get my papers, the journal was gone. I asked the group to look for it among their papers, no one seemed to have it. After people left, I spent an hour searching the room and calling other presenters who had been in the same seminar. The next day when I returned to teach the next session, my journal was lying on the shelf in the same spot where I'd left it.

August 1989

This journal has been out of my hands for a day— picked up by someone else in a split moment of my inattention when I set it down and moved to the front of the room to make an announcement. Gone.

I think I know who had it. Don't know if he read it, but why else was it taken, and why else now returned? I am writing now in this circle of participants, sure that none of them had it. They are too concerned on my behalf, exude a collective innocence. It is the staff which is evasive, eager to step away from the issue. In my mind's eye, I see X standing in that corner of the room, turning his back as I begin to speak. Watch him leave before my session. And so I imagine this book went into his hands . . . the record of my latest thinking about my parents, the transcript from my psychic reading, a rambling sexual longing, notations of when I've had my period, the joys and trauma of my inner life this summer.

I ask myself: how do you feel about this invasion and what have you learned?

First, I'm glad to have the book and pen returned. These are mine, cherished. The record, the page, the writing instrument. Without them last night, I felt as though someone had cut off my arm, severed my story. Second, I certainly feel violated and yet I know I am not really vulnerable and I don't care what his reactions are. I know that he—anyone—who would take this and read it without permission is so twisted in his thoughts he cannot possibly track with me about my life. All his perceptions are wrong, are skewed by the twist in his mind that would allow him to do this.

The more deeply you write, the more you will need to answer the questions in this section and keep considering what kinds of protection and privacy are appropriate for you. Your sense of privacy will change as you become more accustomed to the vulnerability of writing. Over time, writing becomes a more natural activity and you cease to feel as constantly vulnerable as when you started. You put things down on paper that you have never said about yourself, and the page doesn't blow up, the sky doesn't fall . . . you are still sitting at your desk, a little shaken, but able to reread the statements and start the process of integrating these thoughts, feelings, and experiences into your life.

As you can tell from the journal entries you find throughout this book, material that at first is very vulnerable to any one of us becomes less so after time. The journal entries I am willing to share with you I would not have been able to share at the moment of writing because they still represented my most recent and vulnerable insights. No one is cavalier about these insights, but as the journal works to help us make peace with the things which have been burdening our hearts, we expand the areas of comfort out of which we communicate the reality of our lives. This is a great relief. We find out that the real inhibitor to our writing, to our ability to share the stories of our lives, is not in other people's reactions, but in the reactions we have inside ourselves. And so we come to the next issue.

AUDIENCE

Audience asks the basic question: *who are you writing for?* And the answer is never as simple as we think. In the introduction to his book, Thomas Mallon says:

> After reading hundreds of diaries in the last several years, I've come to feel sure of three things. One is that writing books is too good an idea to be left to authors; another is that almost no one has had an easy life; and the third is that no one ever kept a diary for just himself.

We assume that the primary, and perhaps the only, reader of most journals for self-awareness is the writer. Period. No other audience is invited onto these private pages. But our simple declaration doesn't guarantee that we are writing "alone," writing without inhibition, or writing just for the self. No matter how private our writing, we are confronted with two audience-related issues: posterity and acceptance.

The question of posterity is raised because we all know that private papers don't always remain private after the writer's death. Tens of thousands of diaries and journals have been published. Even when they remain unpublished themselves, diaries and journals often serve as the basic research materials for many biographies and family histories. Historical societies, library collections, and attics are full of the private scribblings of the famous and the unknown. Posterity gets dragged into journal writing by the fact that we are creating a tangible record, and by our own cherishing of that record. We write it and keep it; we don't write it and destroy it.

Sometimes, when people write during an especially

painful period and destroy the journal, they often regret destroying the record of their survival and learning later, when the pain is farther away and more manageable. For that is what the journal documents: survival of the self. Journal writing teaches us to value the self, and the self comes to value the records of its growth. It is hard to let journals go. People show up in my classes still grieving for lost and destroyed volumes. Even though the record is incomplete, full of starts and stops and hesitations about our honesty, the journals present a tangible record of life lived. As they accumulate and our sense of audience wavers and changes, we learn to live with ambivalence: the desire to cherish and the desire to destroy. And we put off a final decision regarding their destiny.

When I was sixteen I wrote in my journal for a while to a fantasy figure named Noah. I liked the name, and chose it to represent the person who would come into my life and be my truest love. For another period of time, I addressed the journal as Zoe because it is the Greek word for life. Now there is no addressee at the top of the page, but there is still the ongoing question of destination for these pages, and destination creates tension regarding the journal's eventual audience. I cannot answer this question once and for all. Sometimes I think if the house burned down and all my journals were lost, it would be a relief. Sometimes I think I should go through them, cull what I am willing to share, and cross or rip out the rest . . . but my writing life is not over and I don't know if I have the judgement to make these decisions. Sometimes I think I'll have the journals locked in a vault for a hundred years until everyone mentioned is also dead and my life experience has become historical and quaint. Sometimes I think they'll make a great bonfire of my vanities.

While the question of who you are writing for may never be answered for many of us, what remains important is how we track its impact on our writing. We *will* go through periods of self-censoring details or avoidance of a topic because we are not sure what is going to happen to these journals tomorrow or fifty years from now. We choose to write anyway. We learn to live with the creative tension that draws us to the page, and challenge ourselves to keep overcoming our inhibitions in order to get at the mother lode of our life material.

Audience is also attached to issues of self-acceptance. We may believe that we cannot experience acceptance if we reveal our full selves, but we also desire to test this belief by exposing more and more of our true selves, to the page of the journal, to our own critical judgement, and to others. To understand the connection between acceptance and audience, ask yourself the following questions:

- Who do you perceive as listening or reading when you write?

- Is this listener or reader supportive or critical?

- What are the expectations of this audience regarding your journal?

- What are the expectations of this audience regarding YOU?

- How do you react to these expectations?

- How do these expectations affect your writing?

In a sampling taken at a journal writing workshop,

"the audience" appeared in the following guises for people:

I write for myself, but I'm very critical. It should be perfect, a work of art.

I write for myself, but, oh, my spelling. I guess I'm really writing to my eighth grade English teacher because I can feel him leaning over my shoulder with his red pencil, itching to get into my entries and improve the grammar, spelling, etcetera.

I write to the future, hoping that long after I'm dead, women will read this and that the journals of this century will be valued. It's a new thing for me to even believe in such a long future. I used to think we were going to blow ourselves up. Now I feel like a responsible citizen in the continuum of time.

I write for my grandchildren, things I don't want to share with anyone now, but they may want to know about me in the future.

I write to my own creativity as a writer, using the journal like a pantry where I store ideas. I reach into it whenever I want to work on a poem or story.

There are assumptions, restrictions, permissions, and rules of content implicit in each of these definitions of audience. None of them is "wrong," though all of them affect the writing of the writers. Our ambivalence and beliefs cannot help but affect our writing. In journal writing, we are creating a highly subjective record of our lives. This is all right. It is one of the things we make peace with over time.

Most of the time, I write to the self that is just ahead of me in evolution—the person I am becoming. This "person" carries within her the value system, ethics and lessons of the past, and the amalgam I intend to make of all these things in my future. As my audience, this imagined "person" helps me admit mistakes and take appropriate responsibility; she helps me learn from events and insights, increase in compassion and understanding about life; she helps me make and keep commitments and follow through on my work and play. This internal self is my friend, my "mother," my mentor, my guide. She loves and cajoles me, and gives me the faith and perspective to move on.

Sometimes I can glimpse myself as a very old woman sitting in an overstuffed chair with volumes and volumes of journals piled around my feet. And I am smiling at all I remember that is tucked away on paper, not because it is brilliant, but because its ordinariness communicates human experience.

July 1985

I decided to include the Prague experiences in the Vietnam memoir and delved into my European journals. What a shock! I thought I had written so much more down. What was I doing all those hours scribbling beside one cup of coffee in those little cafes? What is there is good material, though it is written with the skills and perceptions I had as a twenty-three-year-old. Somehow, my memory has kept elaborating—not the details of the story so much, but the understanding of what I was doing there, and the meaning of those experiences. I have to realize, of course, that what I am writing now is just as incomplete, and will seem just as immature as time moves me on from this point, and both my writing and my understanding changes.

When you feel stuck in your writing, look again at the implied audience and the level of acceptance that image offers or withholds from you. Dialogue with your "audience." Change what you need to change in this vision. Work with your taboos, as well as confronting them. Be creative about solving issues of privacy and audience, and choose to let the journal grow naturally. Take a risk: notice what happens to your writing and what you need to do differently for the writing to flourish.

SELF-ESTEEM

Self-esteem is necessary to journal writing. Journal writing increases self-esteem, but we need basic esteem to write and to keep writing. Self-esteem means having realistic respect for oneself. *Realistic* is a key word here. Unrealistically negative expectations ("I can't do anything right . . .") create depression, and unrealistically positive expectations ("I can't do anything wrong . . .") create egotism. One of the potential gifts of journal writing is that it acts as an inner balancing mechanism that keeps us in realistic touch with our self-esteem. Journal writing is a system of checks and balances.

From early infancy onward, we all incorporate messages concerning our self-worth or lack thereof. This assumption of personal value is found beneath our actions and feelings, a constant stream of critical judgement about how we are doing. Critical judgement doesn't necessarily have to be harsh. It may be a voice saying "It's okay. ... You're doing all right. ... This is good enough. ..."

As Matthew McKay and Patrick Fanning say in their book, *Self-Esteem*, (New Harbinger, 1987):

One of the main factors differentiating humans from other animals is the awareness of self: the ability to form an identity and then attach a value to it. In other words, you have the capacity to define who you are and then decide if you like that identity or not. The problem of self-esteem is this human capacity for judgement. It's one thing to dislike certain colors, noises, shapes, or sensations. But when you reject parts of yourself, you greatly damage the psychological structures that literally keep you alive.

Self-esteem will show up automatically in journal writing in how we talk to ourselves on the page. The tone of our communication with the self is very instructive because we have become accustomed to the tone and content of what we say to ourselves, and often don't hear it consciously or register its impact on our attitudes and emotions. For example:

October 1972

What a stupid mistake I made today, talking with G at the office. He wanted me to attend a meeting. I said no because I thought it was a waste of time, and of course, I told him so. ... He gave me this funny look and left. Then I found out from S that *he'd* called the meeting and set the agenda. Sometimes I have no tact at all. And for days I'm afraid to open my mouth, as though it's a virus that must run its course.

Even an obvious diatribe against the self may not be noticed until we enter into a more conscious process of assessing our attitude toward the self. And when an unrealistic attitude veers into self-justification, catching ourselves may be even more difficult because we are not in pain, but are confident and euphoric. *What journal writing helps us do, over time, is discern what problems we are having with self-esteem. By having the courage to write to ourselves in the tone of voice in which the mind is already talking to us, we learn to catch the critic at work and to intercede by replacing old, unreasonable messages with new messages.* Monologue is often the way the mind rants at us. Dialogue is the way to healthy intervention. Throughout the coming topics, self-esteem is almost always an underlying issue: *What do we have the right to expect for ourselves in how we are treated by others, by circumstance, and by our own internalized attitudes?*

Through journal writing, self-esteem changes gradually as awareness increases and new patterns of thought and behavior replace the old. Changing self-esteem requires a mix of gentleness and confrontation. Nobody else knows better than we do, what our minds are saying to elicit the moods we are in from one moment to the next. The mind frames reality, and we see every interaction and experience through the lens of our expectations. It is our responsibility to clean that lens so that a fuller range of options is available to us.

You know what this feels like; we all do. When I notice that my mood has suddenly shifted, I try to sit down with the journal and write out what I'm saying to myself that has caused the shift.

May 1986

Hey, inside there, the sun is out and it seems to be just as fine a day as it was a little while ago . . . what happened to you?

Well, I called X on the phone two days ago and she hasn't called back, so I think she doesn't want to talk to me.

Then I reframe the conversation so that it will cause a new shift, in a more supportive and healthy direction. This is not always simple. But it is a great adventure and a thread of writing upon the page that will give us back much joy.

May 1986, continued

A: I know that you get very anxious when you're not certain what's going on with someone, but you have no evidence that anything is the matter. This is all just fantasy. Why are you already depressing yourself before anything has happened?

B: So I'll be prepared.

A: Be prepared for what?

B: For disappointment, the loss of a friend.

A: Great expectation. Do you really think X is throwing you away because she didn't answer a phone call before your anxiety timer went off?! Would you be willing to not anticipate, and trust me to handle whatever happens when it happens?

B: Yes.

A: Well, would you please go outside and smell the lilacs?

B: Yes!

PS: X called . . . and it was absolutely nothing, not

from her side, at least. So I have one more incident teaching me not to have negative fantasies.

PPS: The lilacs are stupendous this year!

Journal Writing for Self-Awareness

THE WRITING CONTRACT

The following pages are devoted to a series of topics and exercises that explore various areas of content in journal writing. If you are already keeping a journal, you are probably spontaneously writing about many of these things. But some of them may not have occurred to you as topics; or you may find guidelines, examples, and questions helpful to further exploration in the pages of your own journal.

Journal writing is, overall, a gentle process because it is self-guided. *The level at which you ask yourself questions and the responses which come to you are determined by what you are currently ready to know and deal with in writing.* This does not mean you will always be comfortable. Writing for self-awareness implies the ability to increase awareness, and that means living at the edge of your current insight, choosing to ask for more insight. Asking is a risk, and it is how human beings grow. To grow gently, respect your own process and pace, the uniqueness of your life experiences, and the reflections you have about them. There will be times in life when outside events cause you to grow with uncomfortable and dramatic swiftness. To have already developed a root of gentleness in your own writing will help you get through these times with as little trauma as possible and still enable you to learn what you need to from them. *This respect for process is the gift you give yourself, the safety you provide yourself.* No one has a prescribed map you can follow to maturity: we are all making it up as we go along and we learn to notice that the pieces of insight and information we need seem to be there as we need them.

In *Journal of a Solitude,* May Sarton asks, "How does one grow up?" A friend tells her, "By thinking." Thinking is what we all do in order to grow. Thinking is the route to what we need, and the journal of self-awareness can lead us there, page by page. The journal is a way of responding independently to our own particular sense of growth, from a viewpoint of ourselves as healthy, evolving human beings.

Journal writing leads us where we have already decided we are willing to go. We may not be aware of this destination—our destiny—when we begin, but there is a relationship to it that develops in journal writing for self-awareness which is different from other forms of writing. *Journal writing for self-awareness is contractual, a commitment to grow up through the process of thinking, feeling, reflecting, and then acting based on the insights collected from thinking, feeling, and reflecting.* You make a contract to put down on paper whatever you need to record to foster personal growth. Since only you will read this record, you will make subjective decisions over and over again about what the contents need to be, and about how searchingly honest you need to be in this or that moment. The journey of self-awareness does not create a particularly pretty form of writing. It is not often flowery, or even flattering, but it is an extremely effective form of inner-communication.

Going through volumes and volumes of my own journals, looking for appropriate quotes for this book, I think that others would find only about ten percent of the material interesting or even intelligible. Certainly for the decade of my life most deeply devoted to personal growth, when I was struggling through one therapy issue after another with hardly a pause between paragraphs, the vast majority of pages constitute a painful record of sheer determination. Time and again I declared a certain level of understanding to be the final insight, only to find that it merely led to the next level of confusion. Looking back through these pages, I see myself knocked again and again into process, and I know this is still happening in my life, and that ten years from now, I will be able to see the patterns of this moment in the way I can read today the patterns of moments now long past.

Perhaps the delusion that this next insight we write is *the magic one* which will resolve a long-term issue is necessary. As I look at my own journals, I think my contract is that I will use writing to continually give myself hope. Hope that I can make whatever changes and accomplish whatever goals I tackle, internally and externally. The gift of writing is that, while I see the foibles of a belief that keeps proclaiming, "Now I've got it, now I understand, now I'm finished," I also see evidence that this belief is correct to some degree. I do have what I need for the next step and I continue to learn. So will you. And your journal will provide you with evidence of your own journey over and over.

To keep a journal of self-awareness allows you to be an active leader in your own life, to learn from experience in ways that would be nearly impossible without the commitment to reflective and active writing. The journal creates a dialogue within yourself. It provides a forum for asking questions, suggesting alternatives, tracking the path of growth and altering it as you go.

Buckminster Fuller used to say that to be a human being is to be a verb. The journal catches us in the middle of living and lets us see how the thoughts and actions of our lives lead to the next thoughts and actions.

June 1990

I need to find the words, time and energy to have an even deeper level of conversation here in the journal than I have ever had. I need to drop into vulnerable, molten territory, to talk to myself at a level I haven't dealt with before. I need to deal with the most basic elements of articulation. I know what topics are waiting for me to plunge this deeply, but I do not have words for them at the level at which I write. Their words are deep words. I will have to dig. Go underground. Root them out.

To do this, I need to remove anyone else as a possible reader in my mind, the old "what-if-something-happened-to-me" fantasy. And I need to remove the future, to reclaim the journals again as most deeply my own, to formally deal with their vulnerability. I have to separate out, again, my public and private self. To make arrangements to honor the private self and reexamine the habits I have gotten into in writing.

I cannot imagine who I would have become without this forum for talking to myself. The journal has allowed me to interact with my life as it unfolds, to read my progress and catch myself looping back into old thoughts and behavior, to adjust my beliefs and actions because I can see clearly what they are. Hundreds of times journal writers come to me and talk of similar impact the journal is having on their lives, so this must be something that is universal to the act of writing. Writing increases awareness. And increased awareness gives us the opportunity to become and behave as better human beings.

- This self-reliance is especially important *for women*, who from their earliest years are taught to disown their strengths in order to conform.

- This vulnerability is especially important *for men*, who from their earliest years are taught to throw away their weaknesses in order to succeed.

We need to go back and pick up those parts of ourselves that got lost along the way, to claim and celebrate them. Then we may decide how we want to be different, be intimate, be interdependent and active in society.

When we reclaim those parts of ourselves we have been trained to throw away or deny, we experience a rush of self-confidence and power. This rush is the experience of our wholeness returning. There is often a rush of doubt and indecision, too, because we are breaking internal rules we once adopted to feel safe and accepted within our families and communities. Many of these decisions will become more obvious as you work with the topics, questions, and exercises in this section.

The journal is a place to tremble and experiment, to

build confidence in your individuality without having to seek constant approval from others. We may go through periods of imbalance when we withdraw from intimacy with others to reestablish intimacy with ourselves, when we use the journal as a hiding place for all the terror of redefining our once-solid selves. I accept this. In fact, I'm not sure deep change and restructuring can occur without it. But in accepting it I am also determined to have my own growth map within reach—my journal.

PERMISSION TO WRITE

In the interaction of journal writing there is a sense of permission at work that motivates the writing process and provides a framework of topics we are willing and ready to discuss with ourselves. Both at the onset of journal writing and in occasional reevaluations of the process, it is helpful to look at these boundaries of permission and decide where you want your written conversations to take you. To do this, look over what does, and does not, appear in writing. You might start out by compiling a simple list entitled, "In my journal I write about . . ." and then check it out by asking:

- Does this list include a full range of emotions, including those you usually push down or forget to celebrate in your excitement?

- Does this list include areas in which you are still vulnerable and in the process of change?

- Do you allow yourself to appear fully in the journal, making mistakes and being embarrassed?

- Are you humorous as well as serious?

- Do you forgive yourself and others?

- Do you observe yourself learning from experience?

- Are there areas of unspoken silence you are ready to break?

Our personal sense of permission consists of the conversation that we have defined as acceptable or unacceptable. Sometimes there are powerful family or cultural injunctions at work that we may not even be consciously aware of.

While I was growing up, my father's family defined itself as tee-totaling, religious nondrinkers. It was accepted that nobody drank. As I look back from my perspective now, I realize that there were people in the family who drank from time to time, and some of them even developed problems with alcohol, but the taboo was so strong that a blanket denial rested over the whole issue. This left people in lonely isolation, feeling ashamed of doing something in secret, and children didn't develop coping mechanisms or get helpful information about alcohol and its consumption.

One night when I was fourteen, my father came home with what I assumed was alcohol on his breath. I got so frightened that I packed a small suitcase for myself and my younger brother and prepared to run away now that my father had turned from Dr. Jekyll into Mr. Hyde. In the 1990s we live in an age in which alcoholism is a widely discussed social issue, and my example of enforced familial silence seems almost silly. However, it shows how permission and lack thereof functions, first in our lives and later on in the pages of our journals. It took me years to develop what I hope is an intelligent attitude toward liquor, and to write about it in the journal so I could observe my thought process.

In 1960, when my journal writing began, I wasn't, by current standards, saying anything very revealing; however, the taboos of silence that were then still in force were nearly overwhelming. Nineteen-sixty was still a time when we did not easily talk about, or think about, the psychological or spiritual issues we discuss today. I never heard anyone speak openly of alcoholism, abuse, divorce, sexuality, financial or business problems, or any of the true complexities of life. Living in a family where my parents were obviously unhappy, I had no language with which to write about their unhappiness or my own. I believed that everyone else's families were as they presented themselves in public and that we were the only family with a darker, secret reality. When I worked up the courage to mention our familial unhappiness to our minister, he told me it was not my place to talk about it. When I told my best friend, "My family doesn't seem as happy as your family," I cried in shame. There was little evidence that the lid of taboo was about to come off all across society.

Today, when I take this early journal and lecture to high school students, it is obvious that the culture has turned 180 degrees. We have moved from a time when there was no language and no permission to speak or write about many things, to a time when there is nothing these young people can experience which has not already been played out on "Movie of the Week." Now, we talk about everything. And there is a therapy for everything, a support group for everything. We may not yet understand how to really deal with and heal from life experience as we move along, but at least we're talking about it!

Surprisingly, it may not be any easier to find internal permission to write in this revealing environment than it was in the old one. Each of us has to break slowly into topics we have kept silent about and discover our willingness to say what needs to be said.

Many times in journal writing we find ourselves at the edge of our inner permission to write. We fall silent in obedience to rules and injunctions about the journal. If you've ever been in a journal class or seminar, you know that permission expands greatly just by hearing how other people write and noticing what they put in their journals that hadn't occurred to you to put in your own. Permission allows us to add to the range of what we address and the depth at which we address topics such as those which follow throughout this section.

September 1986

There is a tee-shirt fashionable around town these days that has a large silk-screen face of a cartoon woman, hand to her mouth looking horrified. The little voice bubble over her head says, "Oh, my God, I forgot to have children." Looking through my journal as I start another class and lead the discussion in permission, I am as dumbfounded as this cartoon character, for in my journals, I forgot to have sex. I mean, I forgot to make mention of this part of my life. I wasn't having much sex when I started writing at fourteen, and those furtive touches in the dark were certainly not something I'd consider putting down on paper, even if Anne Frank did once mention her breasts on a page of her diary. I never developed the habit of writing about this, and suddenly I realize there's a conversation I need to include here. I am not a virgin.

If you look back at the list of topics you made, you can go one step further by consciously looking for the limits to how you write about these subjects. For example:

- In your journal do you write about what you're doing with your life; *except* when you confront whether it makes sense or not?

- In your journal do you write about sexuality *except* when you uncover questions of how you really feel about your body?

- In your journal do you write about feelings *except* when these feelings border on forbidden zones, such as hate or rage?

For every journal writer, the exceptions and silences we observe are instructive. As we establish a trust relationship to writing, the journal becomes a partner in the process of mapping greater permission. The journal will let us avoid confrontation for a certain length of time, but then suddenly, in the awareness arising from the writing process, our foibles are revealed to us and we must walk them through. New limitations may await our future discovery, but growing confidence in the journal removes their threat, and lessens our anxieties.

The quickest way to remind yourself to push occasionally at the edges of your permission is to write a note to yourself and stick it in the journal like a bookmark. The note can give you permission to:

- Experiment with different topics.

- Stop writing about topics that don't interest or challenge you.

- Try new ways of journal keeping, new exercises, new formats.

MEMORIES AND PERSONAL MYTH

Memory is the basis of all writing. Writing is a way to retain memory and to honor the memories we have. We write things down because that literally helps us to remember them better, and we write things down because writing will help us take a scrap of memory and expand it into a fuller scene or story. Many times people just starting out in journal writing are afraid their memories are so poor that they won't have much to write about. They say things like, "I'm sure there's stuff I could say about my childhood, but I don't remember much." Or they tell me, "The first two years of parenting (or a new job, or the 1980s or whatever) is just a blur. I don't have a specific memory." You will find your memory. You will find it through writing.

Memory is the framework within which our individuality develops. When I was growing up, my mother had an oddly shaped piece of Chinese ceramic she told us was a hat stand for aerating the traditional small black caps Chinese men used to wear. She was very proud of this piece and during the course of raising four children, it got cracked several times. Once, when my siblings and I were gathered together and got to telling childhood stories, we all almost simultaneously admitted to having been the one who broke the Chinese vase. We laughed in surprise to find each of us had taken a kind of guilty responsibility, but when pressed, none of us could actually remember details of the incident.

How we remember, *what* we remember, and *why* we remember forms the most personal map of our individuality. Memory is the foundation of our ability to use the process of journal writing. Week by week as we write the journal it becomes a repository of our memories: as true an account of what is happening and our reactions to those happenings as we are willing and able to record.

Early in her published diaries, Anais Nin examined the tendency for memory to mutate, for us to romanticize our personal past. As a diarist, she valued the attempt to experience life in the moment and to find the layer of story floating just beneath the surface. This transformed reality was more exciting to her than any fiction. The concept of multiple-layered reality creates an interesting tension in journal writing. In her book, *The Novel of the Future, Exploring the Craft of Writing* (Collier, Macmillan, 1968), Nin wrote:

> At one time I was very concerned with my faithfulness to the truth. I thought it might be due to my uprootings in childhood, loss of country and roots and father, and that I was trying to create relationships based on a true understanding of the other person, in the diary as well as in life and in the novels, too. . . . Now I can see that what I sought was a psychological reality and that this reality has a logic, a pattern, a consistency of its own which cannot be invented.

Every journal writer discovers his or her own psychological reality, and the patterns which, together, come the closest to "truth." Writing leads us through a process of peace-making with these multiple layers of reality, and helps us define what levels of fantasy are tolerable, and what experiments in objectivity will be maintained. In all truthfulness, when we write about our lives there is always someone who challenges our memory. This is just a fact of life. We are each prisms, casting the light at a slightly different angle.

Very few things about life are empirically true. There are commonly accepted facts—people are born, people die, people get married on a certain day—but only the feelings and reactions attached to these facts begin to reveal the "truth" about them. In his book, *The Lazy Man's Guide to Enlightenment* (Bantam, 1972), Thaddeus Golas says:

> Facts are limited truths: the way relationships between others look to us when we have limited our own awareness and love, or when they have limited theirs. But facts have roots in the truth. . . . Facts are certainly fascinating, like gossip: who's doing what to whom, what's doing what to what. Of the gathering of facts there is no end. Sometimes we feel that if we had enough of them we could get at the truth.

It is an inhibition in journal writing to imagine we are capable of recording all the facts, or comprehending the full truth of an experience or of our lives. Truth is layered, like an onion. Events take a long time to fully mature and reveal their meaning. The simple breaking of the Chinese vase has much material in it which reveals the dynamics at work in my family—about guilt, about the relationship among the children and between the parents. I may or may not choose to use this incident to explore that complexity, but it is available to me as a gate, and that is essentially what memory is.

Ninety percent of the significance of any event or circumstance is subjective. Subjectivity—the slant at which you or I perceive something—is the basis of our life story. Our subjectivity causes us to perceive certain details, and through the choice of detail we define how and what we remember. Think of the times at a school or family reunion when someone has come up to you and said, "Oh, remember the time when . . ." and you don't remember, even though they do, in great detail. Their map of significance is different. They are telling us something made an impact on them from that time. We have forgotten it because the significance didn't grab us in that moment or in the same way.

February 1983

I woke up and realized I'd been dreaming of Paris, climbing the Eiffel Tower with R. and G. We had reached the top and stood in triumph, looking at the great spokes of the city laid out below. I haven't been there in many years, yet the city stays recorded in my mind. It was so sensual a dream. I could smell the air of Paris, wafting blossoms and exhaust, hear the espresso machines hissing in the backs of cafes, feel the exuberance of being young and poor and proud on the Left Bank. I turned to J. as we woke up, tears of happiness forming in my opening eyes. "I was in Paris!" I said. J. nodded and smiled, but has never been there and cannot recall what I recall. Maybe this is why couples travel, so they can have the same dreams when they are old.

Writers may worry more about consistency, fairness, or objectivity than they do about the essential importance of *subjective* responses. The subjective realm is where the exploration of truth and potential truth lies. The journal is not journalism. It is necessary to give up the desire for empirical truth or complete understanding in journal writing and work toward a sense of building a story that contains all these elements, and something more —insight.

In the journal's record of memory, several levels of life-tracking occur simultaneously:

- What happened as we experienced it,

- The story of what happened developed by sharing our experiences with others,

- The exploration of the significance of what happened that we are willing to examine within ourselves.

  In the journal these three tracks converge, but not so completely that we lose sight of their distinctiveness. Later, reviewing past events, we observe a fourth track:

- Synthesis or integration.

Synthesis provides an explanation, a declared sense of meaning about what has happened and how that incident contributes to the present. Without the journal we end up experiencing synthesis, from time to time, but don't develop an understanding of how we reached it.

After major events in our lives, a decision-making process naturally occurs that works toward this resolution. Consider, for example, the abrupt end of a relationship. We may experience the following patterns of response: First, the journal records the shock of the experience, the facts, and our reactions. We write straight from our feelings: "Ouch. How could he do that to me?" This admitting of an event and the feelings it provokes is followed by a need to share with others, to find some comfort, but also to protect our vulnerability. We shelter ourselves a little from the full force of feeling and the responses of those we talk to. At this point, we talk and write one step removed from feelings: "I told X about the terrible fight Y and I had. I'm really hurting, but it's all right. I'm better off out of that relationship anyway." When we are ready, we re-explore the experience by going back to the feeling level. We begin processing the experience out of a desire for comprehension and rebalance: "Yes, I did love him, and I didn't see the ways we were growing apart. I chose to ignore the signs." Here the journal is excruciating—and invaluable. Entries, written from the instant, record our involvements and do not allow us to deny the importance of our feelings. The relationship as it existed in its heights and depths is written down before us. Eventually we resolve its importance, its termination, its lessons, and are left with an incorporated understanding of this time in our lives. The mellowed synthesis is ready for retelling: "Once upon a time in my life . . ."

January 1974

Once upon a time in my life I loved a married man. And we tried to have an honorable relationship in dishonorable conditions. I was a friend to his wife, a baby-sitter for his children, and a confidant of his dreams. And there was eventually no place we could go with this love unless we were willing to decide. He decided, he thought, for me, and I decided, I thought, not for him. And we broke apart. And he died.

Sunday night, cramped and chilled and unable to

sleep, I think myself back to the day at the airport, what it felt like to press against the window glass watching his plane pull away. I remember running with my sorrow choking me, out to the car, screaming grief and weeping all the way home, madly flinging tears from my eyes so I could see to drive. And I remember hanging my coat in the closet and my brother coming innocently around the corner to ask, "Back so soon?" and I crumpled toward him and pleaded, "Hold me," and thank God he did.

At the end of Chekov's play, *Three Sisters*, Masha bids farewell to the married army officer, the only man she has loved. She will not let go of him and he turns to the spinster sister and says, "Olga Sergeevitch, take her from me." Masha wails and her lover walks with dignity from the yard.

I play each of these roles in my mind: the distraught, the comforter, the one who remains, and the one who is leaving. Our ending was complex this way. The roles crossing back and forth. How deeply I loved him once. I remember the severing, and it amazes me that I seem to love him no longer. I am forced to take stock of that affection, to realize its importance and impermanence.

Through resolution we rebalance ourselves and are ready to move on. We need this comfort after trauma, and only through resolution can we experience contentment with our growing consciousness. The appreciation deepens though when we are willing to remember the process: revisit the passion, indignation, hurt, and confusion, and recognize the pauses in exploration we thought were conclusions. By recording and reviewing yesterday's problems we see today's crises as part of tomorrow's story. In writing the journal from the moment, so to speak, we can observe patterns of survival, learn from experience, and celebrate resilience. We acknowledge the risks of involvement and respect the context of our growth. This willingness to reveal our life-tracking permeates every aspect of journal writing and is its basic celebration.

We have "gotten permission" to carry memories with us to a large extent from our families, according to how memory was valued when we were children and from decisions we made whether or not to remember, for example, things that were painful or discounted by adults, or messages that lowered our self-esteem. We may ask ourselves these questions about memory:

- How far back do you easily remember?

- Were memories treated as important in your family? Did you spend time remembering together?

- Who took major responsibility for carrying family memories?

- How did that person assume the responsibility?

- How did you fit into the remembering process?

- Were there restrictions about what was acceptable to remember?

- How were such memory taboos enforced?

There is much information packed around the answers to these questions. Our response may be a gate, opening us for the first time to the observance of life-tracking. We can record information quickly without stopping to censor or process. Later this raw data is at our disposal in journal work. This primary memory work strikes the tip of the personal and family myth.

Personal myth consists of all the stories we tell each other about ourselves. These are most often colored by an unconscious absorption of cultural and familial guidelines regarding memory, and the responses of others when we have revealed our thoughts and feelings. In the book, *Your Mythic Journey* (Jeremy Tarcher, 1973/1989), Sam Keen and Anne Valley-Fox state:

> In a strict sense myth refers to "an intricate set of interlocking stories, rituals, rites, and customs that inform and give the pivotal sense of meaning and direction to a person, family, community, or culture." A living myth, like an iceberg is ten percent visible and ninety percent beneath the surface of consciousness. . . . At least fifty-one percent of the people in a society are not self-consciously aware of the myth that informs their existence.

Cultural myths are the agreed-upon compilation of subgroup, family, and personal myths. You can start with the macrocosm or start with yourself. Either way, the exploration of myth will provide a map to your journey. In the larger sphere of memory, personal myth indicates the aspects of self or life or existence that we have chosen to emphasize as our primary life tasks.

When I started looking at personal myth, I did it with a simple consciousness-raising exercise. My mother is an Anderson of Scandinavian and Lutheran background and my father a Baldwin of English and Methodist background. To find the myths I carry from these two groups of people, and how I have incorporated them into my individual history, I simply begin a list entitled, "We

Andersons are . . ." and another list entitled, "We Baldwins are . . ."

These lists generate multi-generational stories about work and social ethics, religion and morality, education and intelligence, sex-role scripting, and the relationship between parents and children.

When you work with such lists from your own background, this material reveals the context in which your memory functions, and points out your personal restrictions and assumptions regarding how life "is supposed to be." You may want to expand the lists to look beyond individual and family myths to ethnic, racial and, gender myths, even species myths:

"As an American (Canadian, German, etcetera . . .) I . . ."
"As a man or woman I . . ."
"As a (Caucasian, African-American, Hispanic, Native American) I . . ."
"As a human being I . . ."

Memory is affected by all the things that we are, by all the ways in which we are perceived by others, and by how our humanness has been fitted into a mold that pre-existed our individuality. Knowing what myths shape and guide us is not an exercise in narcissism; it helps us take our place in the planetary community and work within the overall global myth.

September 1986

Just write anything. The point is to wake up and write, to write from the dream outward, to connect the dreaming and waking selves. To allow the moving hand with pen to act as a conduit unperturbed by breakfast or the morning news or feeding the dogs, to discover what story waits below the surface. Experiment. Go.

What do I think is so fascinating about my brother and me during the war years?

It was our war, this one in the jungle with no clear beginning or end. I felt betrayed until I realized I expected our parents to help us, to resolve the dilemma we were in, to intervene; but they couldn't because Vietnam was our war and they couldn't get access to it, any more than their parents could really get access to World War II. At the time I didn't understand their capacity for inaction. Don't all children believe in their parents' willingness to save them from pain?

... We were Hansel and Gretel. Of course, the parents do not intervene, they are the ones who sent the children into the woods in the first place. They seem glad enough when Hansel and Gretel, by their clever wits, find their way home and elude devouring, but the parents do not assist them.

In 1968, the hope I could not give up was that society's parents were going to act in some profound and moral way to stop the carnage. I decided it was my job to state our case so passionately, so clearly, that they would be moved to action. I could not admit we were on our own, or I would have had to look at our orphaning in an intensely personal way. I still had too much need of the broom-maker and his wife to begin that unravelling.

Memory is a jigsaw puzzle of incredible minutia. Psychologists claim we can remember early infancy, or even back to the womb. Present scientific theory views

77

the brain as a receiver of stimuli in the form of electrical impulses which it translates into memories, which, except in cases of cell destruction, are never erased, making even total recall conceivable. However, there is a wide variance among people concerning the depth and range of memory. While science is busy probing the mysteries of our grey matter, we may value memory's function in our growth and enjoy exercising this capacity of our minds.

There are times when memory is overwhelming, and the blocks to memory need to be respected unless you are in a situation of great protection and safety. People who have suffered forms of abuse may repress those memories for decades until something triggers the first recall. **If you suspect you are repressing certain memories, or find yourself suddenly burdened with strange dreams or fantasies, arrange for the help and support you need in order to explore these areas.** The mind is benevolent and has made decisions to repress memory out of the need to protect and preserve you, so do not force yourself. Remember, too, that these decisions to repress memory are reversible, once you have expanded trust in yourself and provided a context of safety for exploring recall. If you become frightened, get support. When you are in a supportive environment, the journal can become a resource you and a therapist use together.

Under benign circumstances, we may exercise memory in the journal by practicing personal remembrances, enjoying the tidbits stored inside us and valuing them:

- What are your first memories of a kitchen?

- What style was the wallpaper in a special room?

- Draw the room plan of the house or apartment you grew up in.

- Draw the backyard or empty lot.

- What paths did you know around the neighborhood? Secret places?

- Write about animals and pets.

- What are your first memories of secret things you did and knew you shouldn't tell your parents? Scoldings?

- What cuts and bruises do your remember? Illnesses and injuries?

- Do you remember the arrival of a sibling?

- Starting as far back as possible, list all your birthdays, Christmases or Hanukkahs, down to the present, remembering something special about each one.

- Pick the face of a loved one and watch the series of still-lifes surrounding that image. Write the first impression of that face and the progressions of memory around it.

- Choose a date—maybe today—go back and try to remember where you were and what you were doing on this date last year, the year before, the year before that, and so on.

The following journal entries show the use of memory in the larger context of journal writing. They illustrate the four stages of life-tracking, mentioned earlier, occurring spontaneously in the journal. They are part of a long-term exploration of childhood that rambled in and out of the journal for many years, just as memory and past experience ramble in and out of present living and writing.

February 1974

In a free association session I go back to Indianapolis, to the house on Keystone Avenue and I stay there for an hour reliving memories of being five and six years old (1951–52). . . .

There is the yard. How big it is. I run in the grass and it's always summer. I help my father in the garden and we squat down, talking about brussel sprout buds. I am repulsed and fascinated by tomato worms, they're so horny and squashy. Dad explains everything to me over and over. I step on a bee, feel the sting and cry. My father's arms comfort me. The sound of his voice talking about bees is soothing. I am not listening to the words.

There is a chicken coop. I love to gather eggs, stooping up and down around the nests. I like the smell of hot shit, hay, and hens. The eggs are magically warm in my hands. I have to be careful not to crack them, because only "big girls" are allowed to gather eggs and carry them safely back to Mother in the kitchen. On Saturdays Dad butchers a hen. I am not scared, but the blood is icky. Sometimes the bodies slip off the fence post and run loose around the yard without their heads. My brother chases them, but he's a boy and littler and doesn't know it's not nice to laugh at a chicken just because it's dead. Do I chase them, too?

I want to help clean the chickens. I especially like the part with all the tiny unlaid eggs inside. I like to feel the gizzard with the gravel rolling around in it. I am standing on a chair at the kitchen sink. It is hot and steamy in the room because a big pot of water is boiling. We have to dip the chicken in the water and loosen the feathers. I don't like that part. I don't like the feel of the wet sticky feathers.

My parents bought me a bicycle, a squat-tired steel tank, much too big for me. I love it. I ride with wooden blocks clamped on the pedals because I am too short to sit on the seat. I know where the worst potholes are on the street and try to avoid them. If I bump through one, the bicycle lurches almost out of my control. I ride around and around our little house. I don't have permission to go very far. . . .

When the session is over and I am invited to return to the room where we are lying on pillows, I watch myself jump on my old bicycle and pedal down Keystone Avenue into the present. I get bigger and bigger until I don't need the blocks anymore. I ride swiftly and with assurance. I pedal into the room, into the woman body and mind of Christina. Ahh, but do I want to come?

This next entry, written a few days later, carries the process of memory into the third track. I am now examining the awareness these memories bring to light, becoming more aware of the patterns of my life.

February 1974

I think my father "got lost" shortly after the time I describe here. I mean, he withdrew emotionally from the household soon after Indiana. Once the family transition was made to Minneapolis he never feels present. In fact, I remember no feelings toward either of my parents for several years, though I'm sure they are hidden somewhere. It is a rather lonely feeling, a sense of always winter. We are trapped together in chill familial tension. When I emerge from this unconsciousness, I enter into immediate BATTLE with Mother.

Test . . . test . . . retreat. Withdraw. Test. I never dare to directly disobey her; I am a good girl. It's something deeper than obedience for which we fight. I struggle to define myself, to withdraw myself from the overwhelming needs and aggression of herself. This may begin at eleven, I think I remember it at twelve. She took me to see the play of Anne Frank, and I started my own diary. It was the beginning of consciousness.

I become the kind of adolescent adults like to have around, a good student, serious, questing, sexually inhibited and blushing, even spiritual. If I am a little overbearing in earnestness, I get praised for being articulate.

I am riddled with insecurities by my peers, almost all of whom seem prettier, thinner, more popular, and existing in a perceived solidarity that twists me with doubts at my own convictions. I counter this scene studying Torah and Japanese, horseback riding, writing diaries and poems, eating chocolate sundaes and making myself throw them up. And every night I spend hours slowly evolving and replaying fantasies of my future that go on for months of development. I am laying the groundwork of myself, and it is more painful than I knew in the process, a time I would not choose to revisit despite its occasional exhilaration.

Later that year, I have moved into synthesis and myth. I am deciding what childhood memories mean to me in the present, dealing both with their power to move and affect me years later, and with the consequences of various child perceptions I was still experiencing as a grown woman.

September 1974

Listen, and I will tell you a fairy tale about myself as a child. Because I made the mother into a wicked stepmother, I made the father into an emperor in new clothes. Because I hated the wicked stepmother, I scrutinized her constantly, protected myself, battled against her influence. Because I loved the emperor, I saw him blindly, adorned in magnificent threads. Only this summer was I able to perceive my need for him to be the perfect parent, the counterbalance to the evil mother. Then I could glimpse a real man standing in his underwear.

I do not know how to relate to the emperor's nakedness because it changes everything, all my fantasies of childhood. Oh, for several years now I've been able to see and accept the human frailties of my father, but I have never before risked having feelings about these frailties. It is so new to be angry with him. I don't know how to touch the man who lives in my mind, don't know how or what to think of the childhood camraderie, the young adult confidences. Our relationship is a string of jewels fallen off their chain. The pearls are paste, should be detected and not restrung. In order to tell what is real and what is false, do I take the hammer to everything?

There are many ways to enjoy memory in the journal. Memory is the layer of richness we spread over our lives like icing. Memory explains to us what things mean, why we have feelings about certain people, moments, or events. I have chosen these particular entries because they are obviously more than simple memory exercises. They illustrate the base that memory provides for other aspects of journal writing. The need to deal with memory, particularly childhood memories, leads to the next topic.

THE INNER CHILD

There is in each of us a continuing presence of the child we once were. When this concept was first introduced in the early 1970s through Transactional Analysis, it was considered a controversial departure from the analytical model which had shaped modern psychology until that time. "The Child" was defined as a separate ego state under the new theory that this internalized being had an outlook of its own and was the source of emotional responses in the adult personality.

Before I ever heard of the inner child as a psychological construct, I was dealing with her spontaneous eruptions and discovering her voice on the journal's page. In my early twenties, during my first years out of college when I worked on the coasts or in Europe and flew home for holidays in Minneapolis, I'd enter my parents' house and find a ghost of myself waiting for me there—a girl-self, needy, restless, and mute.

December 1970

I am the quiet visitor with little to say. The trailing colors from my other world are dim before my eyes here. I am searching for some corner to be mine, for some detail to radiate me-ness, allow me to land with familiarity. I do not live in this family anymore. I have been gone seven years.

Floating around inside me are echoes of all the Christmas Eve days of all the years. I have forgotten how to touch the fevered excitement this night brought me as a child. It makes me want to cry for the little girl lost . . . for the baby lost to the manger.

Who am I? Am I still the young woman who moves with confidence through the work I do, the friends I have? I am suffering from the emergence of that part of myself BK calls "mouse," the lost child, the hidden away child, the self behind all bravado.

When you look at the dates of the entry above and those that follow, remember that they were written at the time when both the culture and individuals were learning to speak about the inner reality of being human in a new way. In 1970, psychology was just beginning to become popularized. The vocabulary and frame of reference which has changed our expectations for our inner lives was then newly developed. Now, we take these new ways of thinking as a matter of course. Psychology has become integrated into our society and our self-concept. I remind us of the newness of these changes because every person waking up to the inner self goes through a period of time when he or she questions whether or not what is happening is normal. In essence, internal awakening forces us to switch to a new definition of normalcy.

In 1431, Joan of Arc was burned at the stake for hearing inner voices. Today, there are dozens of books on "self talk" that teach people how to work with and shape these conversations of the mind. Journal writing for self-awareness could not have happened without this radical change in perception. The widespread practice of deeply personal, exploratory writing is dependent on the availability of understandable and accessible psychological concepts, and popular psychology is, to some extent, dependent on people's willingness to practice personal writing.

I uncovered the reality of the inner child by writing about childhood memories. Time and again, alone at my desk, I experienced an almost tangible memory of toddling steps and skinned knees, the unshakable sense of blond curls turning brown. I reexperienced the physical recording of life from the height of the dining room table. One day, talking with a friend, we began to create a vocabulary to describe the insights occurring to both of us.

March 1974

P was talking to me about her inability to receive, that for her it's a very different function from giving. It feels much scarier, and I asked her why. She said the place in her that gives love is the woman, but the place in her that receives love is the vulnerable child. I say, "It's like a child-hole, everything gets sucked through the facade to this empty place. There is an internal vacuum created. When someone loves us in the present it doesn't stay in the adult woman part of us, but gets sucked into the still vulnerable, insatiable needs of the child-hole." We looked at each other amazed—yeah, that's how this feels.

I don't know how to fix this yet, but I know I need to fill the child-hole somehow if I want to find inner balance and integration. I need to make peace with the past and walk my woman-self emotionally through the child-hole.

It took a while for people to grasp and claim the idea of the inner child, but the concept has been wholeheartedly accepted, especially among people who were raised during the period of silence and cultural taboo, who are now adults in mid-life looking for ways to heal themselves and do a better job raising their own children.

Often they find, as I did, that the first child in need of "raising" is the inner child. And making a commitment to raise the inner child, dealing with our own buried needs, makes raising the next generation much easier.

You don't have to have children of your own to go through this process. The child-self will emerge as soon as he or she believes there is any hope of an adequate response. This is where the journal can help. For it is often in the pages of the journal that the child first emerges, tests your awareness to see if you are ready to understand and respond. A part of you begins posing the question obliquely or obviously: *Do you see who I am? If I come out onto the page, will you help me get what I want?*

Sometimes, it is the adult self, sensing experience being sucked through the present into the past, who begins the questioning: *Who is in there and what do you want? Who has these exaggerated feelings and responses to things? If I talk to you, will you talk back?*

This is the point where the journal is invaluable as a place to write down directly, without censoring, what the various aspects of the personality are saying, and then to engage in dialogue with them. The presence of questions already indicates the presence of dialogue: someone in your mind is asking; someone in your mind is responding. Welcome to a new definition of normalcy.

There are four commitments you need to make to yourself in this area, as a journal writer and as a person committed to self-awareness:

1. You need to *recognize the inner child* as a distinct part of yourself: not the total self, the adored self, or the ignored self, but a real aspect of who you are.

You need to identify yourself as the grownup which the child constructed.

2. You, as grownup-self, need to *develop a relationship to the inner child*. To be able to keep a perspective which is not being pulled entirely inside the child's feelings, beliefs or world-view is essential to being able to help and heal.

3. The grownup-self needs to *decide to fulfill the needs of the child*, rather than allowing the child to try and manipulate others into fulfilling these needs.

4. You need to commit itself to *serve as a protective shield* between the child and the world, and to *negotiate between the child and the world*.

This level of integration is not likely to occur in a week or two. Taking care of the inner child is an ongoing commitment. It will change your life, and change it for the better. There will probably be times when you wish you had never opened the door, because of the fear, the pain, the sense of barely maintained control. Yet this is your hope of becoming a fully functioning adult, a person competent and confident within yourself and in the world.

March 1975

As I get closer to the child-hole the scent of pain rises. Nevertheless, I am determined to enter and endure. It is not healing to sever myself from the past, to seal off parts of myself that are as real today as they were twenty years ago. I see my sturdy girl-self standing in the child-hole in the shadow of my parents and I perceive at last that she needs me.

Chrissie, I ran away from you when I was thirteen years old. I almost remember the day I left you off the train with your bloody baggage and shouted "NO! Don't follow me!" And I thought I ran naked into my adolescence without you. And where were you all those years? Left in my guts, quietly trying to sort yourself out, left alone with the demons. No wonder you feel so scared, who will care for you if I don't?

I'm sitting here shaking my head and crying, for I ended up doing to Chrissie just what was done to her, I deserted her.

And what to do today? . . . Chrissie, Chrissie, come here. I want to talk with you. I want to hold you on my lap and take care of you. You've been strong for so long. Don't worry about this grown-up psychology stuff, you only did what you thought you were supposed to do. You just carried out the messages . . . and you were so brave. I remember all the brave and beautiful things you did. I remember your fantasies and your imagination and your pride. I remember your survival and how much love and chatter you poured desperately into your own small world. Child-self, I love you. It's you and me together from now on. At last.

As the the adult and child voices learn to write in the journal, the challenge is starkly before you: to accept into full consciousness the child's reality and to learn to live as a unified person, able to respond to the inner clamor of your needs and negotiate as a grown-up in the world.

The journal is the place where this dialogue begins, and where much of the work of integration occurs. The journal provides a safe environment for the child to learn to ask and for the adult to learn to answer. This adult, is, in essence, re-parenting the inner child. The next section deals specifically with developing a self-parent capable of meeting the child's needs. As you deepen your awareness and the level of inner dialogue, **please be respectful of yourself, your history, the wounds and misunderstandings the child has to work through, the information and support the adult needs to in order to become a good respondent. Get the help and support you need to make this journey safely.**

Everyone's introduction to the child within occurs differently. The amount of anguish involved in that reunion usually parallels the amount of separation that has existed between your adult and child selves. The process of reunion may be consciously aided in several ways.

First lay the groundwork by enriching your own memory. Begin to experiment with childhood memories. There are ways to enhance your recall and tell your mind that this is a priority for you right now:

- Write about childhood in the third person.

- Address yourself on the page by childhood nicknames.

- Retell family stories and memories as though you were reading them in a book, or seeing a movie.

- Place photographs of yourself around the house: yourself at age two, at eight, at fourteen.

- Look deeply into your face: What do you see there?

- Write down the stories of these periods of your life.

July 1978

She was the firstborn and all her childhood puzzled over the feeling that she'd interrupted something already in progress, but could not see what exactly it was. She learned to walk, making unstable hopping steps between her parents' strides, her arms stretched up, almost out of the shoulder sockets, her tiny hands clasped by the great pillowed palms of Mother and Father. Her name is Christina and this is her story. . . .

Memory can also be aided by asking yourself direct questions and writing about the answers. Don't try to do this all at once. Let memory recall be part of the natural flow of your writing—free associative, mixing the past and the present. This is how the most significant connections are made:

- What do you know about your infancy?

- What was going on in the family at the time you were born?

- How do your parents talk about this period of time in their own lives?

- Do you have a sense of being wanted or unwanted?

- How were you touched and cared for?

- What stories and memories do you have of yourself as a young child? (Include personality traits, specific events, traumas, changes in the family, illness, arrival of siblings.)

- What has been handed down in family anecdotes as important about this period of time?

- What was going on in the wider world during these early years of childhood?

- What impact did these events have on your family and yourself?

- When do you begin to have indpendent memories?

- At what ages of childhood do you see yourself and remember clearly?

- What are your dominant feelings at different times?

- What are your dominant needs? Are these being met? By whom?

- What happened as you entered school years?

- What other people in your life, besides parents, provided for you?

- Were these supportive or unsupportive influences?

- What happened as you entered adolescence?

- Were there changes in family structure, specific responses from adults?

- What questions and burdens were you aware of carrying from childhood?

- What did you do with this awareness?

As you establish a sense of the child's presence and develop empathy with the child, it is possible to become aware of the child's influence in your adult life, and notice the child's voice in the journal. The easiest way to write from the child voice is to *write with the unaccustomed hand*. If you are left-handed, write with the right hand, if you are right-handed, write with the left. The clumsiness of the unaccustomed hand will help you feel six years old again, just learning to write. Do not worry about spelling, penmanship, neatness—this is the eruption of a voice that has been waiting a long time to be heard.

When the journal is written from a state of intense feeling, whether ecstasy or pain, it is the inner child's voice coming through. You will discover that you adopt a childish style, slipping into the awkward syntax, clumsy penmanship, and misspellings of childhood. The child is emotional and works with child logic, which is different from adult logic. The child voice is dramatic, expressive, extreme.

May 1979

This pain feels so small. It says, Come here, go away. I hate you. leave me ALONE. Don't touch me. Do something—make it better. Stop it (the pain.) Stop it (whatever makes the pain come.) Can't get separate from the pain. Get mad at the pain. Hate pain. Hate them (you—whoever gets close). Hate me. I have to suffer. Nothing works. Feel helpless. Hate helpless. Nobody helps me. Nobody stops pain. I will get mad and punish them for not stopping the pain. Nobody comforts me. I can go on being mad, but i am afraid I'll kill them. I 'm sooooo mad, but I'm afraid I'll hurt myself. I'm sooooo mad. They dont care. In our house no one gets stopped from being mad because they are mad and they don't stop themselfs. People can be madder and madder. But I get so mad I scare myself. The only way to not be so mad is to hurt. Hurt bad, so I cry instead of hurt them. Dangerous. Won't show them how angry I am. Won't show them I am danger- ous angry. and then they know i know they hurt me, then they know they hurt me. I want no mor pain and

I want to know how to stay close to good people and not make my feelings big and awful.

It is not important, at least immediately, to analyze the logic of the child; it is important to respond effectively to whatever issue is being brought up. Whether in pain or joy, the child-voice calls out for attention. I bring a sack of crayons and a pad of large newsprint to my classes' dialogue sessions and encourage people to let the child-voice free, *on the condition that they stay equally connected to the adult self, so there is a responsible, compassionate grown-up reading what the child writes, responding to whatever the child says and asks for.* The purpose of the child-adult reunion is to provide a fulfilling relationship, not to repeat old patterns. Often, by the end of these writing periods, people have filled several pages of their journals, or large pads, with crayon scrawlings which are answered in the sedate handwriting of the adult journal keeper: one voice the child's, one voice the grown-up's. At the end of the entry above, the child is asking for help, is saying what she needs to learn. To be respectful of this process in the journal for self-awareness, you need to be ready to offer these lessons.

May 1979, continued

C: You are the one making your feelings big and awful. Why do you do that?

c: I don't know. Aren't feelings big and awful?

C: No, not necessarily. If I promise to pay attention to you, do you think you could have smaller feelings?

c: That's a good idea. You mean, if I was only a little scared, or a little angry, you'd still notice?

C: Yes. I'll try. And if I don't do it perfectly, you

c: could talk to me instead of just making your feelings bigger and bigger.

c: What would I say?

C: You could say: Hey, lady! Notice that I'm having a feeling and stop and do something about it.

c: (laughs) Okay.

Dialogue is the most powerful tool you have in this aspect of journal writing. Use it. Sensitize yourself to times when dialogue will speed up the writing process. Don't leave the child-voice hanging there on the page alone.

At times, I have described the reunion of the inner child and the adult as a process of becoming Siamese twins. We rejoin the severed psyches, memories, feelings, and bodies that we had judged somewhere along the line to be separable. This description is stark, but the reunified self is beautiful, gentle, and adventuresome.

THE SELF-PARENT

The self-parent is the part of us we develop to respond appropriately to the inner child, to fill in the gaps in our development and allow us to proceed in life as an integrated, whole person.

Concepts such as inner child and self-parent were developed to help people deal with an incomplete formation of a mature identity. When I was at college, barely out of childhood and away from the family for the first time, I remember telling my friends that I felt like a piece of Swiss cheese: a person hanging together, but with mysterious holes throughout. I had no name for these missing pieces, and little insight into what I could do about my sense of inadequacy.

Many, many people graduate into physical adulthood carrying a mental grab-bag of negative or punitive parenting, ineffectual or inappropriate nurturing, misinformation, confusion and misunderstanding about who they are or how they're supposed to behave. All this confusion leads people to feel incomplete and inadequate. We have difficulty feeling capable, competent, able to manage our own personalities or behavior. We may not choose to deal with any of this right away, but eventually life creates a kind of reckoning, when the inner work needs to be attended to, and the skills of the journal come in handy.

It took me four years from my first sense of a ghostly child-self, to come up with the working concept of the child-hole, and another year after that before the first greeting between woman-self and child-self, and four more years before the dialogue between inner child and self-parent really began. The journals of these years are filled with increasing determination to re-parent the child and bring my full self into the present moment, able to fulfill my life aspirations as unencumbered by the past as I can possibly become. This is an often arduous journey. The journals are full of pain and triumph, repeated moments when I declare this or that insight to be the one which will unlock my mental bondage to old patterns. There have been uncountable insights struggled toward and celebrated in the journal. Each one of them is an essential part of the process, a building block mortared in place by the act of writing.

The primary thread through all of this, which will be your thread, too, is the task of unlearning and replacing. *You are unlearning all the confused ways you devised to care for yourself, and replacing these old patterns with affirming, empowering ways to care for yourself.* Most of the first years of this journey will be consumed with the need to sort through behavior and thought patterns until you are clear who is whom in your mind, and what pieces you still want to carry with you.

Your goal is to clean up thought disorders in order to develop an integrated personality. There are four commitments you need to make to yourself in this area, as a journal writer and as a person committed to self-awareness:

1. You need to *manage the splintered self.* At first this means being able to manage the splintering: to write in a number of voices, get a sense of the "committee," and record the conflicting messages, beliefs and impulses. This is not crazy.

2. Over time, you need to *undo the splintering.* This occurs as you become less conflicted and more congruent. Congruency means that how you feel, think, and act match in content, that your inner thoughts and outward behavior are not at war.

3. You need to *develop healthy social skills for interacting with other people and accomplishing your goals in the world.* You will probably find yourself changing a number of behaviors that no longer seem appropriate or useful. Integrated people tend to be direct, in both their communication-style and behavior. They are not convoluted because the inner conflicts, which cause convolution in speech and action, have been resolved.

4. You will know you have reached a major point of healing when you can have empathy for your own confusion and empathy for the confusion of others.

In other words, eventually, you need to *give up shame and blame, and get on with life.* By the time you are ready to do this, it will be a great relief, for this is the way the past is lifted from us, and we are finally able to be who we are in the midst of our lives.

Building a congruent, whole personality that can function in the world is no small task. You will not make this journey alone. You need other people to interact with and provide feedback as you test out new thoughts and behavior. Depending on the level of splintering you are dealing with, you will probably want to find some form of professional support. Therapy speeds up the process and provides information specific to your issues. In the '70s and '80s, I used the terminology and support of Transactional Analysis during the most intense years of integration because it was the pioneer theory in this area and what I was studying at the time. By now, inner child–self-parenting theory has been adapted and integrated into many forms of therapy and self-help material.

In preparation for your task as self-parent, you may need to ask yourself some probing questions:

- What feelings do you have about this child?

- Are these feelings authentically yours, or are they the feelings others had about you as a child?

- What feelings are you willing to have about this child?

- How are you going to sort your authentic feelings and reactions from the rote memorization of the feelings and reactions others had toward you?

- If you had to list three things that scare you most about your ability to re-parent this inner child, what would they be?

- How are you going to deal with these fears?

- What kinds of skills do you need to learn so you can take care of the inner one?

- Where and how are you going to learn these skills?

- Is it all right with both of you, if you're not perfect?

- How will you learn from your mistakes?

- How will you reconcile?

- How will you know the integration is working?

In self-parenting, you are creating a replacement for the pieces of yourself that hurt, that are dysfunctional, that cause you to be less than who you are. In general, *a healthy self-parent (and a healthy parent to others) loves the child unconditionally and corrects behavior without shaming.* The parent knows how to nurture and be attentive. The parent listens to the child articulate beliefs and updates them to be congruent with desired outcomes. For example, to create a person with good self-esteem, the parent needs to help the child believe that she or he is somebody important. The parent needs to be powerful. Once upon a time, our parents were the interpreters of the world, and the ones who protected, or failed to protect our tiny vulnerable selves. The world still requires interpretation, and we still need a protector strong enough to shield the inner child from harm, and committed enough to stop the child from hurting him- or herself.

You are not alone in your need to work through

these issues. No human being's childhood needs were fully and correctly met. Everyone has a degree of confusion and inadequacy to sort through. You will have a lighter or heavier dose depending on the extent to which your parents were able to provide what you needed during your childhood, and how you were able to cope with the particular environment you were given. Certainly, there are instances of intentional malice toward children, but the vast majority of human beings are raised by parents who simply do the best they can with the tools they have available, which is largely dependent on the tools their parents had, which depended on your great-grandparents' abilities, and so on back through the generations. Learning to cope with pain, disappointment, and frustration are all necessary skills: it is not just our parents which frustrate us, it is life. We need to know our own resilience.

It doesn't matter where or how you begin this dialogue: it is already going on. Get yourself a basic working vocabulary, pick up a crayon and a pen, and tune in. In the journal entries I use as examples here, you can see the influence of the reading I'd done, but the entries' importance is not in the vocabulary. *Growth occurs in the act of breaking apart the aspects of the self which are in conflict, helping them-me resolve the conflict and putting the self back together in a new, nonconflicted configuration.* The following entry is an early attempt to fulfill the criteria of the parent and resolve conflict through journal writing.

September 1978

Manufacturing anger is done as a defense mechanism by the adapted child. Her fantasy is that by being angry, I will be in a better position to defend myself.

Only what happens, is that I get so angry I stop think-ing: I have no adult available to analyze the problem and no self-parent to protect me. The anger I feel toward others, or toward external situations, is only the tip of the iceberg compared to the anger I dump inward on myself. I bear the brunt of it, and I'm responsible for the whole shit-kicking festival. This time, I'm aware it starts like this:

When someone asks me to do something I don't want to do, the kid gets scared about how to say NO. She believes she has to meet other people's needs all the time in order to be loved, but she's furious that these are the conditions of her life. She doesn't have a way of determining if these really are the conditions of her life, she believes this is true and acts on her beliefs and then the anger comes.

Last night I did a dialogue between Chrissie (the real kid), Miss B (the kid who adapted to all the family messages) and Mama Rosita (a healthy, inner parent) discussing this problem. The problem is that the child has a misinformed belief about fear and anger. In my mind, I sat these two kids down on pillows and let each of them talk about how they respond to fear.

Chrissie: When I get scared I don't know what to do to protect myself. I believe I can't protect myself, so I turn on Miss B to protect me.

Miss B: And I believe that if Chrissie's scared, I'm even more scared, and I scare her into doing whatever the other person wants, or I threaten her that no one will ever love her again—ever.

Mama R.: You two are really good at scaring each other, but you're not good at protecting each other. I am the one to come to for protection.

. . . Mama takes these two frightened girls on her

lap and tells them to stop fighting with each other and scaring each other. She says, "I love you and I want you to let me take care of you and set limits on what you do for other people. You cannot help others unless you let me help you first."

After a while, the two aspects of the child meld into one. Chrissie doesn't need to separate her anger and fear from herself, she just needs to know what to do when she has a feeling. She and Mama R. talk about what kind of grown-up they want to be. Chrissie wants something portable. Here is the image: Christina is a shield, very lightweight with a crystal ball in the middle. Chrissie sits safely in the middle, carrying the shield, Mama R. holds her on her lap. They ride on the back of a lioness.

September 1978: At the time, writing this dialogue felt tremendously significant. For the next few days I was confident that the imagery had integrated a new me. I wrote in big letters: I'm FREE. This was not the first or the last time I proclaimed unflagging belief in my ability to reconstruct myself. Reconstruction takes hundreds of insights, pages and pages of dialogue and discussion. It requires wrong moves, false starts, new beliefs which turn out to be ineffective, pieces of personality that come and go in a changing cast of central characters. You will hear angry voices, sad voices, loving voices, disciplining voices.

In the journal for self-awareness, rebuilding and refining the self is an ongoing process. You can take it fast or slow. After the initial intensity you will be able to proceed on a sort of maintenance program, dealing with self-parenting issues as they come up, while remaining focused on other events and aspirations that you need to write about. You will find yourself on plateaus of growth, contented for a long time, then slowly slipping into a thought pattern or behavior that is vaguely familiar. Then you're back in conflict, again, needing to address the next issue, or the next layer of the same issue.

We are, in this part of the journal, resuming care for ourselves. We cease to hold others—past and present—responsible for the child's well-being, and commit ourselves to direct and caring contact with the inner child. Acceptance of this responsibility will change our attitudes toward our emotional lives. You, the writer, can develop the self-parent by asking questions and discovering the attitudes and skills you have, and those you need:

- How do you hear the child-voice in your present life?

- What is he or she asking for? From whom does he or she want a response?

- How do you attempt to meet the child-self's needs?

- How do you ignore the child-self's needs?

- Which patterns seem to be working, and which do you think need changing?

- Do you know how you want to change them? Does the child know?

- How do you behave now in ways that are reminiscent of the ways you behaved as a child?

- How do you behave now in ways that are reminiscent of the ways your parents and other grown-ups behaved toward you?

- How does the child feel about his or her historical parents?

- How do you, as an adult, feel about your parents?

- Out of which state are you reacting to and interacting with them? (This question is answerable whether the parents are near or far away, alive or dead. It mainly addresses the relationship occurring in your mind.)

There isn't only one blueprint for designing a good self-parent. You build your self-parent in response to the needs and issues expressed by the inner child. This is a *relationship* occurring within the mind. You are building two aspects of yourself which are tailormade to fulfill each other. As you become competent at meeting your internal needs and carrying on internal dialogue, you will experience an increasing overall sense of confidence about who you are and what you can accomplish.

This dialogue does not end. You never stop being a verb, a human being under construction. The depth of conversation deepens. You accumulate a history of satisfactory communication and healing. You have internal trust. In 1989, twenty years after the first inkling of awareness about these issues, I had the following dialogue between child and self in the journal. Notice the increased sophistication. Child and adult think and feel together. The external relationship with my parents has definitely settled down, and the internal relationship is not one of blame, just noticing the conditions.

December 1989

S: Chrissie, I have to tell you are that you are functioning out of a belief that is not true. You did not control your parents into giving you what they gave you; you cannot control the world into giving you what you want. I know you felt helpless. I know that believing you could control them kept you from falling into the terror of living with them, but it was only a fantasy you concocted to keep yourself feeling powerful and sane while you were little. If they had wanted to not provide you with anything, that's what they would have done. You were helpless to stop them; powerless to manipulate them. They chose to keep you alive. They gave you what their understanding allowed them to give you. You were luckier than some kids and less lucky than others.

C: No magic? I had no magic?

S: Nope.

C: I didn't charm them, cajole them, plead effectively with them?

S: Nope. You are charming, and you do know how to ask effectively for what you want, but that isn't what worked with them. Nothing worked with them. They functioned at whatever level they were capable of that day, that week, and that was all there was to it.

C: My anger didn't affect them? My fear didn't affect them?

S: Nope. Look at how ineffectual you have been in the past year when you have had all your power, maturity, and wits about you and still you could not make them relate to you in ways you might desire. If we can't do it now, with all the accumulated skills and insight we have, do you really think you did it then?

C: No, I guess not. They seem better and worse in some ways, though . . .

S: They grow, too. They read. They are influenced by change, including your changes, your getting off their backs and not wanting from them anymore. But making and manipulating don't work.

C: If I give up my fantasy of control, what shall I replace it with?

S: Curiosity. Observation. An open heart that perceives opportunities which also have heart in them, and people who have heart within them.

C: I can do that. But, if I don't really control anything, how do I stay safe? I thought safety and control were the same thing, or were hooked together. That's what it looked like.

S: It's too bad you didn't get the chance to feel safe when you were very small, because I think it is this experience which teaches children the difference between safety and control. If you had felt safe, when you were only a baby, then you would know safety exists in the world, long before you were big enough to even think about the idea of trying to control . . .

C: Bad things happen. People get hurt. We all got hurt.

S: Yes, that's right. And you and I are taking all this hurt and learning from it. Spiritually we are always safe.

C: I understand. They never felt safe, either. They didn't know how. They scared me all the time, because they weren't really in control. There was no sense of control. But that household

doesn't exist anymore, you and I exist, and
God, and we're all safe.

S: Yes.

The concept of self changes, matures, integrates. You
won't need to write forever in the child-parent voice,
though their dialogues keep the journal conversation
vibrant. You will find room and energy for expanded conversation, greater awareness of the world, the chance to
write about a wider variety of topics, and the need to
bring your current relationships to the journal for reflection and considered action.

FRIENDSHIPS AND
PARTNERSHIPS

It's true, what all those nonjournal writers suspect of us:
we *are* writing about them. It's impossible not to. Unless
you are living in total isolation, there are other people in
your life who affect you and create situations about which
you will feel the need to write. Relationships offer
moments of celebration and trauma which become part
of the tapestry of the lives that we record on the page.
This often creates a great deal of confusion, and sometimes paranoia, both for the writer, who ponders what he
or she has the right to write, and for the people involved
with journal writers, who wonder what is being written
about them.

First, *to the journal writer*: You have the right to write
whatever you need to, the assumption being that there's
a reason for putting the details of your relationship with
others down on paper. Sometimes the reason may be to

express your love, sometimes to sort out and learn from your anger, hurt, and confusion. The purpose of journal writing for self-awareness, after all, is to experience insight and growth, and our relationships are life's testing grounds where much insight is offered and growth occurs. *Journal writing can greatly help people in relationships because it offers a neutral place and a private forum to get clear before and after personal interactions.*

Next, *to those who know journal writers:* Your life story is not being disgorged onto the pages of other people's journals; *their* life stories are. Journal writers write down their own lives. You are part of their lives, and they mention you, but you are not the central focus, they are. If you want to know more about how this works, start keeping a journal yourself, and you will discover what a thoroughly self-centered activity it is. It's a healthy self-centering, but there just isn't time to write everyone's life. Over and over again, journal writers have to opt for telling their own lives, and for talking about the aspects of what's happening that are the most gripping at the moment.

Most of the time, we don't really "write about other people." We are writing about *our perspective* on the relationships that we're involved in. This is different from what others may suspect we're doing, and one way you can reassure family or friends is to talk to them about the self as central character in the journal and encourage them to develop their own centering technique, whether it's journal writing or something else. Back in 1974, I was aware of this while writing about a friend.

October 1974

I see M almost every day. She stops by for tea or we take a late evening study break and talk on the phone. But I feel our "time" has just disappeared into law school and her man traumas. I am frustrated at how to "get her" to be a good friend to me when she has so much else on her mind.

We are good friends. We love each other. But I have time on my hands and want to spend it with her, she has no time on her hands at all. She has committed herself to an expensive and consuming course of study. When I admit to myself, and to her, that I know my frustration is my own, then our situation becomes liveable again. After listening to myself talking to her, I decided I'm becoming stilted in the way I approach her and how I behave when we are together—as though there is nothing she can do that will quite satisfy me. I don't like what this does to us, to her feelings or mine.

Journal writers benefit from having a private way to discharge the emotional energy that relationships often create before practicing on another person. The purpose of writing is to get clear about our own thoughts and feelings, to explore what is possible and realistic in any given relationship, and to let go of unrealistic expectations. The woman referred to as "M" is still a close friend. Over the years we have cycled through many expectations about each other and adjusted to changes in our lives: career changes, partnerships, widowhood, successes, failures, and the long haul of keeping to our life paths. It's good to have a friend along who's known me so many years, who knows the private stories and hidden pains that are part of every person's progress. As problems have come up between us, we have chosen to combine the sharing of friendship with the privacy of writing and reflection, so we could make contracts and connections with each other that have remained satisfying.

- Who are you writing about besides yourself right now? Make a list of your cast of characters.

- What do you wish you were saying about them that you're not?

- Are there ways you want to present a more balanced picture of your relationships?

- What do you need to write that you're not writing?

- Are issues of audience and privacy being churned up when you write about others?

- Are there ways you need to clarify your audience again, or reclaim and protect your privacy?

The more closely you know someone, the more likely their presence in the journal is assumed without explanation. People come and go in the journal without introduction and sometimes without farewell. I do this, too. I have always thought that as long as I am writing these pages for myself, I know who the characters are and don't need to explain. However, I recently came across a lovely card written to me by "Sue" in the early 1980s. She wrote to thank me warmly for dinner and for our meaningful conversation. I had taped this card to the journal page, because it is beautiful and because what she said touched me. The only problem is, I don't know who she is anymore. Which Sue did I know then and have over for dinner?

As a result of this mystery, I write out at least once in the margins, the full name and meeting circumstances as a new character appears on the page, what our relationship is at the moment, and whatever else seems appropriate. This forgetfulness is not senility. It is not callousness.

It is not anticipation of future researchers combing through my journals to identify the cast of my life; it is simply an acknowledgement that I have already lived a long time, and intend to live longer, and that I have warm, intimate moments with people which are genuine but do not necessarily lead to long-term relationships.

In the book *An Interrupted Life*, (Pantheon, 1983), Etty Hillesum's published diary of the war years in Amsterdam, the editor has placed two pages of numbered notes:

1. For some time Etty had felt her life needed sorting out and firm direction. In February 1941 she consulted Julius Spier, the S. of these diaries.

3. Liesl Levie. She survived the war and now lives in Israel.

7. Frans is unidentified. Reijinder is a café on the Leidesplein.

39. Johanna Smelik, daughter of Klaas, not to be confused with Jopie Vleeschouwer. "Jopie" is a nickname given to both sexes.

44. It is not known to whom Etty wrote this or other letters here which nave no addressee indicated.

A form of such notes is helpful, even for ourselves. When we are living the moment, our interactions are vivid and we don't anticipate ever forgetting—but we do.

Friendships and partnerships are both chosen relationships. The purpose of writing about others is to better understand why we have chosen them and why they have chosen us. We choose people because we sense the possibility of an exchange that we want or need. I need a friend; you need a friend. I want someone to talk to; you want someone to talk to. I like to play Scrabble; you like to play Scrabble. We are attracted to certain other people, and they are attracted to us, and that attraction forms the central mystery of the relationship as it unfolds. This attraction is the contract between us. Some psychologists theorize that the contract that sets the tone and direction of a relationship is exchanged in the first four minutes. These first transactions are a blend of body language, verbal exchange, intuition, and compatible understanding about what we each seek to learn next. We may be surprised, if someone articulates this contract too clearly or too quickly, because it removes some of a new relationship's mystique. But the contract is there. And the contract has been there since the first meeting. I remember the moments when I met several close friends, and each greeting had its own character. As you respond to some of the questions raised here, you can discover the contracts and assumptions which fuel your relationships.

The journal's role in friendship is often to help you ponder what the contract is, to update it as you each change and grow, and to keep track of the many invitations for relationship that occur daily:

- What do you get from your closest friends?

- What do you give in return?

- What do you think the original contract was?

- What do you think it is now?

- Can you or do you talk about the contract between you?

- How do you validate your friendship?

- When was the last time you started what feels like a significant new friendship?

- Does the contract seem different than it would have if you had started this friendship a decade ago? Different how?

We need to be in relationships with other people; it's part of being human. A human being alone and isolated has a hard time not going mad. In stories about survival in totally isolated circumstances, the struggle to remain sane is as primary as the struggle for food and shelter. Other people give us feedback on an essential level. We see ourselves through the reflections offered by others. Mirroring is a mutual exchange. It is not always an easy exchange, and because we have a tendency to write about what is unsettled and troubling, there may be more troubling things said about others in your journal than praises. You can change this by deciding that it's worth your time to include the sustenance and good things you get from and share with others.

July 1989

Had another great talk with C today. I am so lucky to have her in my life. She is willing to be interested in a lot of the same details I keep working out and clear that she's not just going to blindly take on my point of view, or take my side in something. I like our boundaries, as well as the ways we are close.

November 1990

Well, S and I are going to be friends. We've known each other as business colleagues and been excited about the ideas we generate thinking aloud, but not open to each other's dreams and life goals the way we are now. All this changed in one conversation. Nothing dramatic, just an opening into the possibility that we might be able to offer each other something more, and the mutual realization that we wanted to. It's as though we were sitting on one level and dropped quietly through to another level where we regarded the other differently and said, "Oh, that's who you are . . ."

A relationship with a partner, the person with whom we want to spend a significant portion of our lives, often has the most intricate contract and the longest list of expectations, assumptions, hopes, and disappointments. We are not only sorting our own confusion, but cultural confusion. Our families have modeled these relationships for us. The times we live through model these relationships. Television, movies, books, stories, and mythology all emphasize the significance of love partners, of husbands and wives. And we carry emotional baggage that we cannot know is in us until we enter a partner relationship. We discover our expectations through trial and error, through finding out where we are compatible and where we suddenly experience trouble. There are lots of jokes about who squeezes the toothpaste tube the right or wrong way, and how to unroll the toilet paper, but anyone who's been partnered longer than six months knows these are not the real issues. We are trying to sort out what's important to us from this load of personal and cultural baggage, and what we are ready to discard.

January 1982
My father came to visit us the other day and was talk-

ing, obliquely as he does, about some of the struggles he has in his marriage. I tried to think of something useful to say and told him, "You know, it took me several years, but I finally decided I wasn't ever going to get P to use the 'right' amount of dish washing soap. I grew up trying to make these little essentials stretch as far as I could, and I still apply Depression era stringency to every bit of soap, toothpaste, tissue, etcetera. But I can't change P who believes the dishes aren't clean unless a certain amount of soap is squeezed in the water. Once I decided to stop struggling about these stupid little details, things have been calmer in the kitchen, and more peaceful in my head."

I expected my father to get this simple point and to understand he might be happier if he wasn't criticizing K in his mind all the time. Instead he ranted on and on about how we each have to take responsibility for polluting the planet and if I couldn't stop P from excessive use of the soap, we were all going to die . . . or some such escalation. I was dumbfounded and stumbled out of the room, but as I think about it now, it makes me laugh and makes me sad. No wonder I have a tendency to get in these ridiculous power struggles, I learned from the master. I'm supposed to spoil the days of my relationship over a teaspoon of liquid soap and ignore the megapollution that occurs elsewhere? This is an important point, Christina, watch yourself and weed your behaviors!

The poet Rainer Maria Rilke said that love is when "two solitudes protect and touch and greet each other." In the solitude that continues even in the closest relationships, we are able to explore our individual sense of reality, responsibility, and view of the world, instead of assuming that what another thinks or believes is more important than our beliefs, or assuming that our view should be the dominant one. The privacy of the journal is a healthy format for this solitary search. Many good relationships contain two journal writers who work on their life issues and expectations alone and together:

- In your partnership, the one you have, one you have had, one you hope to have, what are the contracts?

- How much of this were you aware of when entering the relationship? (Look in your journal, if you had one, for records of what you wrote.)

- If you were to write a contract now, what would you say?

- If your partner were to write a contract, what do you think she or he would say? (Of course it would be a good idea for both of you to do this exercise.)

- What are the expectations you had about marriage or partnership that you have had to give up?

- How have you done that? (Are you both doing it?)

- Do you have ways to talk about these things? Do you have ritual ways for setting aside old expectations and celebrating together?

- What do you think the primary lessons are that you are learning from each other?

- What are your primary joys?

- What are your primary griefs, disappointments?

- Overall, are you happy?

These questions invite an uncensored appraisal of what you are up to. If you will make a commitment to answering them as honestly as you can, they will help you live more authentically with yourself, your partner, and your friends. Uncensored appraisal means that you ask yourself hard questions that challenge your social conduct, that you are willing to be uncomfortable on the page, so that you may be more comfortable in the company of those you love. You need to be willing to know what your contracts are.

- Are you invested in giving to this relationship, or only getting?

- Are you really interested in this person or are you using them because they are convenient?

- How might you be leading yourself into a future mess?

- How might you be being led into a future mess?

- What does he or she want? Is that what you want?

If you are terribly frustrated with a relationship or individual, there is something the matter with your expectations. You may have unrealistic expectations and are meeting resistance from the other person; or perhaps you have realistic expectations, but the connection you want is not available with this particular person. The journal becomes a sorting ground for understanding the multiple layers functioning in almost every human relationship.

When I look back at many entries over the years, I see the same kind of long-term sorting about how to become a good partner, a good parent, a good friend, a good teacher, a good business colleague, that I saw in trying to build a good inner child–self-parent relationship. The journal is full of insights, declarations of my own understanding, and the dawning awareness that I have more to understand about this complex dance of interaction. In the journal, I read through years when I tried to change others, instead of looking at whether or not what I wanted was possible. I read through years when it didn't occur to me that I could leave unsatisfying relationships and find new people who wanted to provide what I was asking for and wanted to receive what I had to offer.

You know what questions you need to ask yourself in any relationship: they are the little gnats of thought that occur in the shower, in the car on the drive home, or after you get off the phone. You may brush them away quickly because they interfere with the momentum of what's happening, but they are intuitive flashes and you need to pay attention to them. If you dare expose yourself to your own intuition, and if you have safeguarded your sense of privacy enough to protect against imagined or real intrusion, the journal can be a place to talk honestly to yourself about relationships.

Journal dialogues are a meaningful writing tool in sorting relationships because you can tap insights. Dialogues help you see the "gnats," and discover what you are thinking to yourself, just below full awareness. Say, for example, that you want to explore the nature of a cyclical fight you experience with your partner. This fight has many sources, some little thing between you triggers it off, but after a few minutes, you realize that this is the same old argument, no matter what the topic. You may even be able to say to each other, "Oh, here we are again, having fight number 11-B." But you—probably both of you—feel trapped and can't seem to get out of the fight until it's run some kind of course. This pattern is a mystery to you.

In the journal, you decide to write a dialogue about this fight. It is not important to record the cycle word for word; what you are looking for is some way to break out of it. Before writing, neither of you consciously understands what dynamics exaggerate these little arguments until they feel like major struggles. So, in the journal, you hire a part of your mind to be the overseer, to watch both of you have this fight on paper and to intervene, ask questions, help you get to the layer of insight. Perhaps you are afraid that if you give in ("Okay, use all the soap you want . . ."), your partner will lord it over you, the way someone in your past has treated you. And perhaps your partner is afraid that if he or she gives in ("All right, I'll only put a quarter inch of toothpaste on the brush . . ."), he or she will look weak and you will ridicule him or her. In the dialogue, when you uncover the fears and assumptions that drive each of you, you can then go to your partner and ask if this insight seems accurate. Or, the next time you start this fight, you can interrupt it and ask for the reassurance that will break the cycle of assumptions. ("This is where I always get stubborn. If I concede the point here, will you promise not to treat me the same way my father always did?") In such ways, the insights of journal writing help us make better relationships and teach us where the line is between what our minds assume, and who our friends and partners actually are.

This is one of life's long journeys. Relationships change constantly as the circumstances around you change and clarity expands within you. Be patient and compassionate toward yourself and each other. Help each other learn to think and write and solve problems, and the journal will become a tool that your friends and partners honor for the benefits they see it bringing to them as you become more fully yourself, and more fully their companion.

RULES AND BELIEFS

It should be fairly obvious by this point in journal writing, and in reading this book, that *our lives are run by internal rules and beliefs*; they may or may not be very helpful to us, or even have much to do with external reality. People are defined as crazy if their internal beliefs and corresponding behavior become so far removed from what the rest of us consider reality that they cannot function, or become dangerous to us or themselves. And yet no one has an objective view of reality; everything we perceive and think is filtered through our belief system and through the rules which tell us how to apply this belief system in the world. This filter is called a frame of reference.

If you look back at the section and the writing you did about personal myth, you will see some of this belief system coming to the forefront:

- What *are* you supposed to be like?

- What will your family think of you if . . .?

- If someone wrote out your life as a script, what would the script direct you to do?

- What if your life were a fairy tale, what kind of adventures would you have? What would the moral of the story be at the end?

- What messages were given you indirectly about how to conform in order to fit in your family, in your subgroup, in your society?

Whether you know it or not, you have rules for everything you do, and everything you don't do. You are not crazy for having these rules and beliefs; they are an unavoidable part of the human psyche. Journal writing exposes these beliefes both obliquely and directly. As you look through the entries you have written, you will eventually begin to see the beliefs and rules which guide and drive you. They are the journal's pentimento coming to the surface.

A term from painting, *pentimento* is the presence or emergence of earlier forms which have been painted over, but now bleed through the surface so the original strokes show through. We all have mental pentimento, rules and beliefs we think we have painted over, until we find ourselves in a cycle where we are paralyzed by them, bewildered about why we cannot do what we know is in our best interest to do.

Adult life confronts us with situations for which we have no ready belief, and therefore no coping mechanism, no handy response. Adult life also presents us with situations in which our beliefs look ridiculous even to ourselves. I can think of a number of times when I have taken on too much, and needed to reestablish priorities and back out of certain professional, social, or volunteer commitments, and it has been nearly impossible for me to decide what to do. I have been paralyzed by what would be a fairly simple decision since I had carried, for many years, a confusing set of beliefs about never letting anyone down.

Most of these life-driving beliefs are not laid out clearly in the mind. They are incorporated into our thinking and embedded in our actions. The only way we know we have stumbled across one that no longer works is by our incapacitation, and it may take us some time to even notice our incapacity, because that, too, is incorporated in the rules we follow about how we respond to a request which goes against our beliefs. In the pattern I described above, I don't seem to have comprehended that I was taking on too much because the rules did not include a healthy warning system or sorting mechanism. The answer was always, "Yes, sure, no problem . . ." By the time I got to overload, I was practically at physical collapse, feeling trapped and desperate. And all this had to do with trying to live up to expectations I had picked up somewhere along the line, to please teachers now long retired, and parents moved to other states, and bosses, friends, committee members who had no intention of creating havoc in my life. Until I could see the rules and believe that I had a right to change them, I was stuck in my own unconscious behavior.

Journal writing for self awareness is a form of ongoing housecleaning of our rules and beliefs. Through writing we may become aware of what rules and beliefs we are following at any given time. Then we may ascertain whether or not these beliefs and rules are functional:

- Do they provide good options?

- Do they allow you to respond to changing circumstances and requests?

- Are they flexible and accommodating (and not overly accommodating) of other people?

- Can you change your mind without going through

long loops of guilt, anger, anxiety, explanation, excuses?

● Do you feel able to negotiate on an equal basis with other people (not taking a position one up or one down)?

● Can you make mistakes without shaming or blaming yourself?

● Can others make mistakes without your shaming or blaming them?

● Is your learning curve relatively painless?

● Can you alter and update a belief or rule and use it effectively?

● Can you adopt rules and beliefs you haven't used before, that look good to you?

To operate in our lives effectively, and to have relationships that are caring for ourselves and others, we need to clean house about what we think and why we think it. Going after the underlying beliefs can be subtle. The entry below looks like hundreds of entries I've written over the years, and like entries you may have written, too. To get at the beliefs governing our thinking and behavior, such entries have to be reread and scrutinized.

April 1977

I've been home from New York for two days, and I'm angry, confused by my anger. I have lunch with K, a nice conversation, but I float in and out. On the streets of Minneapolis, I jaywalk and dodge traffic, try to whistle for a cab—and none of it's really there. It's not that I wanted to stay in Manhattan, it's that so much has happened in the past ten days, I cannot return to my life as I left it. I feel repulsed at my life. I am home, and business as usual is waiting for me and I don't want it back. I don't want so many people demanding time and energy from me. I don't want the intense conversations in which I end up feeling enveloped in the other person's space. R called to say we have a lunch commitment for tomorrow, where are we meeting, and I feel "How dare you assume to penetrate my reentry!" At first I set up time with her, then, after an hour of angry resentment, called her back and told her I'm not ready to break the solitude. That really causes me to think about how I'm going to take care of myself. All I want is time to write uninterrupted by teaching, by publication publicity, by trip planning, extraneous conversations. Everybody wants a piece of me, and I want a peace of myself!

The beliefs which caused this sense of time crunch are obvious to me now, years later, and may be obvious to you as an outside reader. If you are going to sleuth your own beliefs, you will need to work with past journal entries, so the issue is not immediate and you can understand the lace of beliefs:

- Choose entries which contain unresolved feelings.

- Read them aloud, slowly, listen to what you are saying.

- Ask yourself: What beliefs are driving this situation?

- Ask yourself: What change in my beliefs would change my sense of options?

The reason our beliefs are so confusing to us is that they were picked up accidentally in the midst of various historical moments, most of which we no longer remember, or inherited through family and social systems, or absorbed by osmosis when nobody intended to pass them on. The commitment we make, in the journal and elsewhere, to ongoing mental housecleaning is what leads to maturity. *Maturity is being able to decide what we believe, based on deliberate decisions about what has meaning.*

> October 1982
>
> I got a call for another speaking engagement: Could I please come to such and such church and speak to their women's group. . . . they can pay me twenty-five dollars. I didn't get angry. I didn't guilt myself. I just said no. I am committed to talking to women about journal writing; and I am committed to taking care of my time. It occurs to me, that if I value my time, if I say to this well-meaning lady, who probably has a husband supporting her, that I make my living this way, and twenty-five dollars a morning is not a living wage, then maybe she will think differently about her own time's value. Maybe she will find more than twenty-five dollars to offer the next speaker. This is a touchy area, because I don't want to exclude women who can't pay, but I am tired of speaking to groups of women who look like they're living a lot more comfortably than I am, and who are hearing me for free, or for a sum that is so small it's meaningless to them.

Redeciding a belief may at first sound contrived, an activity that will be strange to us, but it's not. We update our beliefs all the time. Once, you believed in the tooth fairy. Once, you believed that stepping on a crack would break your mother's back. There are uncountable beliefs that pass through our minds; some of them stick, some of them don't. A lot depends on circumstances. If nothing ever happened to your mother, even when you got mad at her and went outside and stomped on all the cracks in the sidewalk until your anger was spent, and tiptoed guiltily home, afraid to look in the kitchen until you heard her bustling about, unaffected by your revenge, then this belief came and went without much attachment. But if, in a bizarre moment of fate, you stepped on a crack on your way home from school and arrived to find an ambulance in front of your house because your mother fell down the steps and broke her ankle, this belief will become entrenched in your mind. Even years later, when you can rationally explain the coincidence to yourself, an aversion to cracks, or a heightened sense of superstition may still plague you. And you will have to dig through your psyche until you understand the cause. *Once you arrive at the root cause, the spell of a belief can usually be broken, the rules amended or abandoned, and you will have liberated another part of yourself to autonomy.*

When I was a toddler, my father liked to do acrobatic tricks with me. I stood in the palm of his hands. He swung me around in a large circle over his head. My parents report that I seemed to like this activity and there are photos of me, both serious and smiling during these wide arcs. Years later, trying to break free of a layer of the inner-incorporated father, I remember experiencing intense fear, strange muscle tension, and an irrational expectation that I was about to die. I wrote and wrote in the journal, extremely puzzled and uncomfortable. Finally I reached the insight that released me from this perplexing pain.

February 1981

I am sitting in Aunt Gin's rocker, the place in the house that feels the most sheltering to me. I have been here an hour, most of that time sitting on my hands because I have this irrational urge to plunge my fists through the window, and I have promised myself I won't move until I know what this struggle is about.

Daddy. Daddydaddydaddy . . . I keep dreaming of myself as a baby again, of playing with Daddy. He is swinging me around, his little acrobat. We perform for their friends. All the grown-ups laugh. I laugh, too, because it must be funny. It must be a game. Am I scared?

I got out a photo of myself, eleven months old, standing in the palm of his hand, high over his head. I must be seven feet off the ground. What if I fell? Didn't anybody worry about that? Did I worry about it?

Shit. Now, I'm crying . . . that's it: If he lets go of me, I'll be dead. So the kid decided: If I let go of him, I'll be dead. Child logic: the converse must also be true! No, I will not die if I let go of my father. Let go of the man who lives faraway. Let go of the ghost who lives in my head. Not dead . . . ALIVE.

New belief: the more I let go of my "father" the more I will be alive. This is my power mantra. Now I can get out of the chair.

Recovery from addiction provides a good model of how beliefs and rules can affect our lives negatively and positively. In addiction, people deny that they are addicted. People tell themselves over and over that they can handle their addiction, whether it is to alcohol, food, drugs, sex, or dependent behaviors, but they fail to handle it. To recover, they have to give up this belief. Finally, they become ready to admit they cannot handle the substance or behavior. This is the statement of a new belief.

The First Step encapsulates the change in the addict or dependent's frame of reference: "We admitted we were helpless . . ." By admitting this specific helplessness, people are freed to find and experience new beliefs and rules which will return self-esteem, build success, and help them lead integrated, powerful lives. *Empowerment comes from changing the focus and the belief* from, "I can handle alcohol." to, "I can handle recovery." The change in this pivotal belief, leads to many other changes in belief. Working the Twelve Steps is form of mental housecleaning. In a repeating cycle, people go through a life-changing process. The journal is like that, too—we finish an entry, but never the book.

To work your way through your own intricate maze of rules and beliefs, start by making a list in the journal of areas of your life: career, family and friend relationships, money and prosperity, spirituality, religious faith, health, and self-care:

- In what areas, by your own definition, are you successful in applying your life skills?

- In what areas, by your own definition, are you unsuccessful in applying your life skills?

Choose an area to work with that is most intriguing to you. Work with the successful area first:

- Define success: What is happening that is satisfying to you?

- List the beliefs in yourself that foster and support

this success (Be as specific as you can, writing nuances and near repetitions is fine).

- List the rules that govern your behavior that foster and support this success.

- Where did you learn, or make up, all these beliefs and rules?

- If they were not handed down to you in such auspicious, functional form, how did you adapt them so you could succeed?

Now work with an area that has been less successful:

- Define failure: What is happening that is unsatisfying to you?

- List the beliefs in yourself that undermine you (Again, be as specific as you can).

- List the rules that govern your behavior.

- Where did you learn, or make up, these beliefs and rules?

- Since they don't work, what is causing you to hang onto them?

Compare your lists. Think about what you have done to increase success and change your beliefs so that you achieve more success:

- Are there ways you are empowering your beliefs in failure?

- How are you doing this?

Instead of defining yourself as a failure, become curious about this process. Become your own private detective in your mind. Scour out vestiges of this or that rule, this or that belief. Write it out in story form, in dialogues, in outlines and maps and mazes. Be like the white rat who will not give up and will find his way to the center of the labyrinth, eat the grape, and be free.

Every time you succeed at something, jot it down in your journal. Use red ink, or write in the margins, make asterisks and stars so you can find these points later and can trace your experience making change. Build successful change upon successful change. Start small and keep sleuthing.

DREAMS

It is well established in scientific literature that everyone dreams, though not everyone remembers dreaming. Dreams, like most functions of the mind, respond to attention. If you proclaim, "Me? Nope, never dream," you will assuredly avoid remembering dreams. If you wait passively to see what happens you will only occasionally remember dreams. And if you ask for dreams, prepare to write them down, and later work at interpreting them, you will remember them and develop an insightful relationship to them. This discussion is intended to whet your appetite for dream-catching. My statements and ideas regarding dreams are culled from many sources and experiences that have attracted my attention over my journal writing years.

Dream interpretation has been a part of human cultures from the moment we sprang into consciousness. Dreams and their interpretations are woven into mythical and spiritual stories, legends, literature. The ancient Greeks went to the Oracle at Delphi to dream. Kings consulted their seers about the meanings of dreams before taking political and military actions. With the onset of analysis, Sigmund Freud shifted dream interpretation from the mystical to the psychological. His theory was that dreams reveal our most hidden desires, forbidden sexual and emotional fantasies that are taboo in waking life. Freud's early disciple, Carl Jung, took the insights of psychology and reintegrated them with the mythic tradition. He developed the concept of the collective unconscious by researching universal dream symbols that appear in dreams of people all over the world. Dreams which tap the collective unconscious involve archetypal figures such as the Wise Old Man, the Great Mother, the Inner Friend, and the anima or animus, as well as other symbols, images, numbers, and colors that Jung found to be universally interpretable. Edgar Cayce, a psychic and pioneer of dream work in the West, had dreams that revealed past lives, gave premonitions of the future, warned of illness or revealed its cure, or described astral travel or other occult phenomena. Fritz Perls, the founder of Gestalt therapy, emphasized the potential of dreams to work out inner struggles. The recent writings of psychologist Ann Faraday note the great ability of dreams to help us solve problems. And Patricia Garfield provides directions for creative dreaming, in which our waking mind may direct and request certain specific information from our sleeping mind. No matter how you want to think about dreams, they are helpful pieces of knowledge and insight to include in the journal for self awareness.

Unlike waking thoughts, dreams occurring while we sleep do not leave a memory trace on the brain. For this reason they are the most elusive of our memories. To catch dreams we must be gentle with them upon waking and ready to record them almost immediately. Once we have reconsidered dreams consciously, they become thoughts and are recorded in the mind as such.

To catch your dreams, wake naturally, or put an alarm clock (never a disc jockey's voice on a radio-alarm) where you don't have to leap across the room to turn it off, and keep paper and pen at hand. Upon waking, remain as still as possible and listen to your mind for dream snatches. As soon as an image arises begin constructing other fragments around it, even if it seems to be the last or middle part of the dream. Jot down whatever you can reconstruct: a phrase, name, place, sense of what was happening. A quick sketch of a dream scene, even a rudimentary one, is as good as writing the dream down in paragraphs. I can look back through old journals and see a sketch of stick figures and funny-looking trees, and still remember both the essence of dream action and how I interpreted it. You may remember more dream fragments in the course of the day and be able to build a fuller sense of the dream story. Unless there is something in your dream so compelling that you can't proceed with the day until you've processed the night, you can wait a while until you have time to work with interpretation; but try to get at it before you sleep again, because the next night's dreams will dull the vividness of this one.

One of the most effective tools for recalling dreams is simply to start reading about dream work, and to expect to remember them. If you do not remember dreams as you would like, recite to yourself before going to sleep: "You are my dreams and I have a right to you. I will remember you, treat your messages with respect, and explore further." Then date the paper by your bed and, confidently, fall asleep.

September 1986

It's been over a month since I wrote here (dream journal) and it's not laziness. I've been going through one of those times where the sorting is so deep I don't remember anything in the morning. I know I have dreamed, but before I can catch it, the images are gone. Fragments.

1. I am with Peter O'Toole in *Lion in Winter*. We are outside, woodsy setting, mirror hanging on a tree branch, putting on ceremonial robes, makeup. We must walk to the castle, but first have to cross a deep channel filled with water. We plunge in, walk through up to our necks in rushing water.

2. A high school, large crowd of kids, feel like I did then, not sure how to be part of the group. Gym is filled with orange and black balloons which I am trying to keep inflated with helium. Three giggling girls come up to me. I tell them, "No one is interesting who hasn't been through hell." They stare, this is not what they expected me to say. I am thinking—it's true, better get used to it.

The pattern of dream inquiry presented in this section combines Ann Faraday's work and Gestalt and trust in your own intuition. You are looking for resonance. This concept, as defined in Faraday's writing, states simply that *the correct interpretation of symbols will resonate, or ring true, as you discover it.* References in dream books may list the interpretation of symbols, but don't accept that interpretation until you have tested it against your own resonance. What Jung says a bluebird means, and what your unconscious says a bluebird means on a specific night in early June, may be very different. Trust yourself first.

I don't read dreams books much anymore. I did notice that when I read Jung, I dreamed in Jungian symbols. When I read Faraday, I dreamed in Faraday's symbols. The mind wants to communicate, and will talk to us in whatever language it thinks we are most likely to understand at the moment.

Dreams and dream interpretation come into the journal in many different ways. Dreams may show up in flow writing. They may be integrated parts of memory entries or records of the day's activities. You may find yourself being influenced by the news or other events, and starting to write about waking life slipping into sleeping life, or the other way around.

November 1968

I dreamed that Euene McCarthy won the election. He came to Macalester to announce his victory. We were all going mad with excitement, except Dr. L, who's a republican, and about ten students. I saw PD pounding his fists against the bell tower. He kept saying, "He will ruin this country. He will ruin this country." Finally I asked him what he meant. "Peace," he said. "It's a crumby idea." I was absolutely shocked to think I had dated him, and he has such a twisted mind.

Of course, when I woke up, I realized that the PD's of this country have won again. Who could have voted for Nixon? Living in San Francisco, I forget what the rest of the country is like. We are in a fairyland here, and I love it. But when I leave the city to speak, which I do a lot, I feel as though I'm crossing a border as real as a national border . . .

When you are ready to interpret a dream, repeat it aloud to yourself telling it in the present tense. Let your-

self get back in touch with the action and symbolism of
the dream experience. After that, you may want to ask
yourself a few basic dream questions·

- Why are you dreaming this dream now?
- Are there symbols in the dream whose interpretation is obvious to you?
- Are there symbols in the dream that you remember from other dreams?
- Are there symbols that reflect your activities, interactions, or even the television programs you've been watching during the last few days?
- Are there any puns in the dream?

When necessary, go through a dream, symbol by symbol, until you understand it. The following dream took
some detailed work to unravel, but it illustrates several
journal techniques that can be applied to this process. I
recorded it in the present tense and read it aloud before
working on it.

January 1988
I dreamed I was in love with a man named *Howard*
who was a junkie: We live in a big flat in the inner city
and he's started using again. His *best friend, a doctor,*
is also addicted. *A crack dealer* comes and offers us
lots of money to let him turn the flat into a crack
house. We have a scene in which I am yelling at H and
the doctor, trying to get them into treatment.
    Rest of dream is at *Hazelden* (Treatment Center).
H and I part, he goes to treatment. I wait in the parking lot with other wives and families. After treatment

H comes out. I *hug* him, we hold tightly onto each other, sobbing with *heavy emotion*.

I ask each underlined symbol in the dream: *Who are you, and what are you in the dream to tell me?* They respond:

MYSELF: I am the part of you that wants to get on with the journey and feels weighted down by Howard.

HOWARD: I am the disowned part of you. I am addicted to laziness. I think there's a shortcut to wisdom.

DOCTOR AND FRIEND: I am your own willpower. I try to keep H in line, but I slip into his beliefs, instead of convincing him of mine.

CRACK DEALER: I am all the ways you could get turned aside from the path, not accept discipline.

TREATMENT CENTER: I am something larger than all your selves. Everybody needs to come to me, to surrender to Higher Power.

HEAVY EMOTIONS: You, self on the journey, know you must help H. When H comes out of treatment, you can integrate and become one whole, strong self.

After this much interpretation, I decided to take the next step and do a dialogue between Howard and myself.

ME: Boy, would I like this struggle between discipline and laziness to be over so I can just get on with my life.

OVERVOICE: So, where do you think you and H are in the process?

ME: We bounce around. Sometimes I'm still

ranting at him, sometimes he's in treatment.

H: The problem is, I'm not the problem. Our disintegration is the problem.

ME: I agree. I'm willing to stop making you the problem. I'm willing to love you, see you as part of me. All my feelings in the dream have to do with my longing to be at one with you, but your lack of attention prevents that.

H: You love me, but you want me to change.

ME: I want your belief that there's an undisciplined way to live a spiritual life to change. I'm willing to change, too.

H: How?

ME: I'm willing to become you.

H: I'm the bad one, the no good one. Nobody has ever offered to become me before. Do you really love me?

ME: Yes. I don't know why, but I do. I'm willing to give up my fantasies about how pure I am, in order for us to integrate and go on.

H: I'm willing to give up my image of how bad I am, stop trusting myself more than I trust God, and go on with you, too.

Not every dream gets this kind of attention, but after a while you will develop signals that flag dreams containing the more important material coded within them. If a dream wakes you up, if it is repeated, even in variations, if the image hangs with you all day, pay attention. These are signs that your unconscious has a message for you.

SENSUALITY AND SEXUALITY

We are inundated with sensuality and sexuality in this culture. In the media, in advertising, in books, and in huge cultural controversies, we debate the meaning of sensuality, sexuality—what is erotic, what is exploitive, and where the lines should be drawn. There are fanatics on all sides and people whose experiences and ways of self-expression seem strange to us, no matter what our proclivities. In the midst of all this confusion, I think that most of us are just trying to be at home. To acknowledge that we are physical beings, figure out how to take good care of ourselves and how to experience pleasure in ways that fit our values, circumstances, shifting energies, and changing priorities.

When I taught journal writing in grade schools, I developed an exercise called the *ME Page*, which I now use with adult classes, too. One section on the *ME Page* asks people to draw five parts of their bodies that they like. From fourth graders to fifty-year-olds, there is usually some giggling when writers get to that suggestion. It makes me sad that we are so easily embarrassed, that it's hard to think of just five things we are willing to admit we take pleasure in, enjoy, or admire, about our bodies.

Obviously, this is an area where rules and beliefs abound. And the journal, again, provides a safe place for sorting these things out. On the pages of the journal we can come alive to ourselves, talk out our confusions, heal from and celebrate past experiences and behavior, and decide what we want to carry forward. This sorting is necessary because we are changing all the time. What felt right or appropriate ten years ago may not feel right or appropriate to us now, and social circumstances have changed as well.

Our sensuality is the range of physical response we allow ourselves to have with the world. It is the pleasure bond, the open channel between our personal energy and energies around us. Through sensuality we experience the flow of emotion between ourselves and others; we notice the textures of the things we touch, the taste of food, the temperature of the breeze, the heat of water showering our nude bodies. Sensuality functions all the time, because the body takes a constant physical measurement of its reality whether or not the mind is focused on it. Shift your attention for a minute from this page to your shoulders: are they stiff? relaxed? They were in this state a moment ago, whether or not you noticed. *Sensuality is the choice to live in the body, to be aware of life in a fuller sense than the mind alone can give us.*

Limitations on our physical awareness begin in a psychic circle extending beyond our bodies three to four feet. We tend to live enclosed in shells of "personal space" and habitually raise or lower our guard at any encroachment. In the increasingly smaller physical spaces in which many of us live, these private territories are violated constantly and throw us into a state of tension whether or not we are aware of it. And when someone encroaches onto our territory—even benevolently—we may refuse to break our shells and reach out to touch and respond. We end up censoring our perceptions in order to protect this psychic bubble. We suffer from this censoring. To explore our sensuality, we must often begin again with the basic awareness of ourselves as bodies within a physical environment.

- Remember days on the beach when the sand was so hot it was like walking in ankle-high ovens?

- Remember sitting so high in the apple tree that the wind took you, limb and all, in its sway?

- Remember the first snowfall of the year?

- Remember the taste of hot fresh bread and honey, and how you ate half the loaf before you noticed?

- Remember the first time you kissed someone?

- Remember?

Well, I remember. And I write it down in all its glorious, celebratory detail.

May 1990

Saturday morning: The sun rises out of the Atlantic, shining straight into the condo living room, making the pen a shadow across the page. B found a wonderful condo, all sliding glass doors and screens which face the sea, just above the dune so there are palm fronds and bracken in the sight-line over the balcony, and then the long stretch of beach, and then the sea, and then the sky. We can walk for miles in either direction. Bands of morning clouds lie above the water, pink and dusty blue. The sunrise is mottled like the empty oyster shells I find along the beach. The sound of the sea is a constant roar. I have been sleeping and living with it, love the thumping constancy and beat of calm. Wherever I end up living by the sea, I want this sound and rhythm to fill the house.

Sensuality is an awareness that comes giggling and skipping out of the natural inner child. Sensuality is a sense of wonder. There are ways to use the journal to raise again our awareness and celebration of the senses. If we are separated from such perceptions we may ask:

- What do you see, hear, feel, taste, smell, right now?

- How aware are you of each sense? Which gets the most attention?

- Where is your body touching the environment right now?

- What did you observe sensually about the people you met today?

- Who and what and how did you touch today? What response did you get?

- What did you eat for lunch? Did you taste it?

- What details do you notice first when entering a new environment?

- What do you notice first about other people? What do you think they notice first about you?

- What is happening to the trees today?

- What would your house feel like if you were a cat? a dog? a bird?

The list is infinite. It can be playful or serious. As you write about sensuality, you will discover not only the things that give you joy about being physical, but also the things that bring you pain or add to your confusion. Once again, **be respectful of yourself and your experience. If you uncover areas of abuse, get appropriate support and counseling.**

Bodies, our individual bodies, are the basic instruments of sensuality. And bodies, individual bodies, are where many of us begin censoring our acceptance of ourselves and our environment:

- Where did you learn your body image?

- How did your mother feel about her body?

- How did your father feel about his body?

- What family rules did you live by regarding touching, affection, nudity, sex?

- What was the family vocabulary for parts of the body, bodily functions, sexual acts? What did these words imply for you?

- How did you get touched as a child and by whom?

- Were there traumatic instances connected to your early sexual awareness? Have you worked to resolve them?

We have a body fetish in our society. The women's and men's movements have raised awareness of the messages each gender receives about their bodies. Almost no one seems to think that he or she is attractive enough, not even people that are held up as the ideal. We read of actors and actresses, models and sports figures who internally do not believe they are beautiful, in spite of unremitting adulation. Too bad . . . for us all. For unless we believe we are beauty-full, we hesitate to touch others and be touched in return. To be ecstatic about the world around us we must perceive ourselves as ecstatic creatures. Hiding within our bodies, we are separated from sensuality and spontaneity. *To really accept the beauty of the world, we must have a place in ourselves that under-*

stands our own beauty, that accepts the experience of beauty and ecstasy from within. In the journal we can examine the relationship with our bodies:

- Well, how do you look to yourself?

- What five things do you like best about your body?

- Are you getting touched ways you like? Do you experience comfort and pleasure living inside your skin?

- Are you not getting touched in ways you don't like? How are you going to take better care of yourself?

- What are your confusions about boundaries? (Follow the rules and belief section exercises.)

- Can you see the source of your comfort and discomfort with certain parts of your body, and how you are touched there?

- What are you going to do about getting your touching needs met when you know what you want?

- How do you want to reach out to others that is different from your present behavior?

Once we have a grounded understanding of ourselves, the world opens up around us. In the journal we move again and again from the inner to the outer, reunifying ourselves with the intricate sensuality that surrounds us.

Flow writing is a good exercise for exploring your sense of wonder: conjuring up fantasies about ant hills, recording the touch of evergreen boughs, watching a candle burn down to its base, perceiving the subtle daily changes in weather. Writing that is based on sensuality, on our experience of ourselves in the world, is some of the most pleasurable writing we do.

May 1975

On the sidewalks of my hill a thousand tiny fading blossoms are lying face-up in the rain. My heart catches. I am not ready to let the lilacs go, though they fall and brown as carelessly as they came, bursting one by thousands into visible fragrance.

I am disconsolate not to have lived in the alley, camped out with my Chinese quilt and a pot of English tea, playing most purple songs all night on dulcimer and recorder. I am remorseful not to have plumbed their excuse to be excessive, to weep great tears, to laugh giddily letting the whole scheme of things strike me as ridiculous, to dance Dionysian madness on all the winter's bones. Lilacs, lilacs— these were my grapes and wine, and nothing else the ripe year offers for drink is quite as sweet.

But I have drunk them, motif of my coming down, coming home to center again. Lilacs led me to some goodbyes, to some hellos, led me in and out of old love's longing. And Friday night I found a bush someone had pruned with the blossoms still cluster full. I carried home an armful, set out two huge bouquets and filled my bed with the rest. Late, after midnight, I lay naked and luxuriant in my self-created, self-nurturing bower. The dog sniffed disdainfully at my romanticism and headed with a sneeze for the foot of the bed. And I was expecting no one, just loving the lavender freedom, just loving myself at midnight.

Sensuality, in the normal process of physical and psychological maturing, leads to awareness of sexuality. And sexual awakening leads to a life of decision-making about choices, boundaries, ethics, how we define ourselves, how we define others, how we want to spend our time, and what impulses and desires get the most attention at the moment.

Sexuality is like sensuality; it's there in the body and our choices are about how much and in what ways to pay attention to it. Each person makes ongoing choices about what kind of relationship he or she wants to have with this life-force that lives within us.

June 1975

Something on the beach. White, limpid, looking ocean-logged, inert. Slight movement. In the pubic seaweed a finger beats the ocean's rhythm on the sheathed pearl. It lives.

First day of my period. Cramps. I wake and go through the perfunctory motions of masturbating, a few mild comes to urge the clots out, to relax my tense uterus and lower back. I am not turned on. I am not relating to my sexuality, not relating to this womanly function. I feel just as I've described myself— something limpid, washed up throbbing on the beach.

And I am angry at MEN. Angry at R's intrusion into last evening and the scent of the hunt that hangs over him. I am angry at my indiscretion, telling him the flat above me is vacant. I suddenly have this image of a huge unwanted prick being laid over the protected womb of my house. R is on the prowl and I don't want the hassle of having to define boundaries in the household. I laugh bitterly.

Last week L sent me his long-promised erotic letter. I am strangely complimented that he will share its rawness, that he will share the vulnerability attached to his penis. He says, among other things, that he wants to take all femaleness into his lap and fuck all women. In later conversation I tell him, "It's a different fantasy to be penetrated by mystery rather than your imagined penetration of mystery. If I want to penetrate you, penetrate men or maleness, the only point of entry I have is your head, the way you give me entrance into the spirit of you. The male body does not provide a corresponding genital opening that the woman can take, nor a way to feel her most private part of self being all encompassed, held, accepted in a male vagina."

He laughs, then turns serious. And we are stuck here again, aware of each other as foreign countries. We sit on opposite ends of the couch like a map of Europe and don't know how to continue the dialogue. So, again I feel alone, something tossed up on the beach.

In the journal we may explore, both in direct question-asking and in accidental rambling discoveries, our feelings about sexuality:

- Is there a definite line or a blending between sensuality and sexuality in your feelings? Is this appropriate to your life-style and needs?

- Are there parts of your body where you feel your sexuality is focused?

- Do you treat these parts differently than the rest of your body?

- How do you get "turned on"? How do you keep yourself from being "turned on"?

- Who is in charge of your sexual feelings? Where did you learn these attitudes?

- What do you usually do with your sexual feelings and do you want to change these responses?

- Do you have (or feel the need for) friendships where you can talk about your feelings about sexuality?

Sex is not something confined to the pelvis. Sexuality includes the entire body and awareness of life energy. Sexuality expresses our desires within an understanding of all that we are, and all that our choices make us. And when we accept it, our natural eroticism flows more freely in the journal and in our lives.

February 1989

I dream of women kissing. And when they kiss they are transformed. I kiss another. Sometimes a stranger, sometimes a friend drawn into my mind for the night. Our lips touch fire. This is sexual. We want more. I reach with light-filled fingers and caress her cheek, her hair, her forehead eye. She places her hand on my high heart. Her hand sinks into my opened breastbone, softened like a pillow by her touch.

This is sexual, but not the way the movies show it. Not the way men dream of women, or women dream of men. This is purer than anything I was told I could know. Our lips smile into each other's mouths. Something sacred comes and we are not confused. We admit we are angels. We whisper "maybe" and leave small boats for sailing in the eye.

Sensuality and sexuality are the animation the mind gives to the body, the integration of physical and spir-

itual energy. Our bodies are not ours forever. What a shame it would be to have them and never experience their wealth.

GRIEVING AND LETTING GO

Life equals death, for life is change, and in every change something dies, something ceases to be as it was. Death equals life, for death is change and in every change, something new occurs, something that was not before now is. This is the great riddle. Its mystery moves through our lives constantly. Its process moves through every aspect of the journal.

Death takes many forms: deaths of childhood as we assume adult roles, deaths of friendship and love relationships, deaths of marriages, deaths of the parent-child relationship as our children's definitions of our place in their lives evolve, and deaths of the child-parent relationship as we ask our parents for shared adulthood. We experience the death of certain expectations about ourselves as life molds us in one way or another and we confront limitations in our abilities to grow, to change, to excel in careers. And death also comes to us as death, the final letting go that emerges out of life's littler deaths. People we love will die before us and people who love us will watch us die. It is a form of self-love to prepare for and accept these experiences. We need to contemplate and accept death and to practice grieving. Grief is a lifelong companion in the life of any person who is awake to change. And grief is not such a hard companion to travel with along our road.

Grief is the emotion which finishes things. Through grief, we flush clear and become ready to absorb the next experience. When we grieve a loss, we create space for a fulfillment. When something we have longed for is fulfilled, amid the celebration, we will also grieve the end of the struggle, because there is change. Over time, I have come to believe that the presence of grief is a very good sign, an inner blessing that signals my aliveness as deeply as sensuality signals aliveness. Grief is the emotion of the survivor—the whole person.

Grief allows us to resolve past experiences through the synthesis process discussed in the section on memory. Grief allows us to let go of the hurts in the child-hole as we pursue the dialogue between the child and the adult self. Grief is an aspect of risk taking in relationships, in changing beliefs and adapting new rules and inner guidance for our lives. Grief appears in dreams, to invite us to heal, to let go, to resolve issues or estrangements that we may not be able to heal in any other way. Grief is an aspect of sensuality and sexuality as we explore the aging of our bodies and perceive the great and mysterious mortality in the world moving around and in us. Whatever experiences life offers us, we need to accept and celebrate and grieve them and to integrate grieving into our being until these little deaths become acceptable parts of our history and of who we are.

June 1988

I went to my twentieth year college reunion this past weekend. In anticipation, inducing a kind of reverie, I've been driving around playing 1960's tapes in the car. Deciding to attend these functions always raises for me the question of *why* I am attending.

When we are children, parents will choose a door-jamb or closet wall, and measure our growth year by year ... I have grown immeasurably in the past twenty years, and it is much more complicated to measure this intangible growth. Maybe my college reunion is like standing against the doorjamb so that I can see myself at twenty, and see myself as I am now. This measurement is never something my classmates and I seem able to discuss openly. Conversations turn in unexpected directions, are broken off as people join and leave the cluster, go back to the buffet and never return. Many split-second decisions are made about trust, about personal revelations, how much we will let these essential ghosts glimpse our current lives.

At the end of the evening, I stood a moment alone in the courtyard by the humanities building, trying to remember what it felt like to be the college girl who went here long ago. I see her photo in the yearbook. I remember a few stories about her. But the emotional reality has been replaced by all the experiences since. What we still have in common are books, the river of words, certain sudden longings that can sweep over us listening to Simon and Garfunkel, the Beatles, Joan Baez. I feel so full, and so grateful to be alive, to be standing in this dark summer's night at the end of the party, who I am. I cry, but it is not grief alone, it is a wondering acceptance. Chrissie—Hello. Goodbye.

Life's intermediate deaths are not always easy to perceive. Sometimes the only way we may know a death has occurred is through awareness of grief. In learning to perceive the grief process we may learn to decipher the change that is causing it.

Grief consists in three major stages. The first stage is *shock*. Emotional shock has certain things in common with physical shock, such as the denial of an injury. A man may break his leg and hike down off the mountain before feeling pain. A widow may make all the funeral arrangements and remain a charming hostess to family and friends before she stands alone, aware at last of her irretrievable loss. You and I might have a phone conversation with someone, and an hour later realize that the temperament of the day has changed, and have to spend some time in the journal, tracing grief back to some subtle hurt or change that occurred over the phone.

January 1987

I got a letter from X Foundation. I didn't make the finals. This doesn't surprise me that much. I guess I don't expect to get support from them, my work is borderline literary as far as they're concerned. The only reason I even apply is because of that cheery slogan from TDP: "You can't win the game unless you're in it. . . ." so I try to keep a-devil-may-care attitude about it all.

(later) Been depressed all day anyway, and seriously considering whether or not I should even apply for these things. They drive me crazy . . . or I drive myself crazy with low level hope and high level disappointment.

The second stage of grief is an overwhelming sense of the consequences of an event and a *hypersensitivity* to the disruption. We are as yet unable to fit the experience of loss or change into our view of ourselves and our lives. During this time the grieving person goes through periods of inertia, anger, sorrow, and denial of the new situation, and the process is even further complicated by a sense of having been betrayed by the person who died or the situation that changed, or by the fact of death itself. Family and friends who do not seem to grieve similarly may be objects of many unresolved feelings. If you are feeling super sensitive for a number of days, one of the appropriate questions to ask yourself is whether or not you are grieving.

May 1973

Suddenly in the rush of B and D's wedding I remember what I felt like on the day J left me that August. The intervening time does not shield me from full memory of those twenty-four hours and its impact on my life.

I came down to Iowa to be their bridesmaid. Last night, long after midnight, I sat on the sleeping porch watching my bride-friend toss in her dreams. And I wept silently into the wedding napkins, feeling myself an estranged older woman. And today, after the light tears of happiness for their beginning, I am again overwhelmed with the business of my grief.

Now, riding the bus back home, my heart is broken open like a red tulip falling apart, exposing the black base to the petals and the yellow unmet stamen. I cry and cry. It rains and rains.

I remember myself in love and mourn what I have become since. I relive the shock of suddenly finding myself a woman alone instead of his partner. I was so emotionally committed to being at his side, I cannot absorb that reality ripped from me. Why is today as hard to live through as all our other partings? Where are my protections against this hurt?

The final stage of grief is *resolution*, and it is perhaps the hardest to understand. Resolution doesn't necessarily lessen the impact of loss and change, but we reach a point where we are able to incorporate the experience into our lives. We do not get over grief, we walk through it. We cannot fully understand the process of resolution until we have dealt seriously with grief ourselves. Our expectations for recovery that precede grieving are very different from the resolution that emerges inside grieving.

April 1990

M called this afternoon to tell me R died a few weeks ago and to recite the story of his passage, the seven weeks he lay ill and letting go while their children gathered and the family healed through the act of his dying. It was a true Tibetan rite of the dead.

The whole time she was talking, the image in my mind was of our times in Chicago years ago, when we would spend a Saturday afternoon in their sun room massaging each other. As M spoke of his death, I worked on R's great barrel chest, seeing M and myself pushing love into his body and the smell of oil and the heat of sun on our backs and flesh under our hands. Ours was never a traditional friendship, but it worked with great ease and safety. The boundaries could be blown out wide, and we stayed safe.

A long thread of my life passes through my mind while we talk. She sounds well, still in a kind of sacred shock to have been so long with dying. We hold years and years of memory for each other and I believe she will find this new stage of her life fulfilling once she can claim it. I want to tell her about L, how the mystery of death is its presence and absence combined. But she will find out in her own way.

Whether it's a transition or a literal death, there is most likely something you are grieving right now. The journal for self-awareness causes so many changes that grief becomes a steady companion of the writing process:

- What are you grieving right now?

- What stages of grief are you in regarding different experiences?

- What griefs have you resolved that have become an accepted part of yourself and your history?

- If you dialogued with grief, what do you think it would say to you?

- What lessons have you learned from grief that you might not have learned any other way?

We emerge from the grieving process changed people, people who carry the reality of our experience and our grief forward with us into the rest of our lives. While the change is occurring we may temporarily be isolated from easy social contact with people who do not understand grief or who have their own expectations for our resolution. In the journal we find a place that will accept all our feelings. In the journal we find a place that does not impose rules of acceptable behavior, acceptable duration of grief, acceptable changes during grief. The journal absorbs our labor with grief and honors our survival and return to life.

As our lives move further and further in time from a major grief experience, we become aware that no one besides our inner self knows the whole story. We become aware of an awesome process of synthesis moving in our lives, which grief brings sharply into focus. We may still be intimate with people, but we will always carry a private understanding of ourselves deeper than we can communicate. And the journal becomes the place where we acknowledge the special privateness of our being. I have discovered that I knew this even years ago. From my vantage-point now, I would say that I had yet to suffer what I have had to suffer since. And when I am old, I will feel the same way about who I am now. Suffering teaches us to stop suffering; that is its lesson.

August 1975

I spent the evening on the porch with a close friend. We were planning new activities for autumn and suddenly I remember, it is three years ago that J left. I have not been watching for this anniversary, not anticipated the annual rolling around of this date. And I think: if I had known how unlimited life would become beyond that sadness—how eagerly I would have gotten underway with my grief. And I think: if I had known how long the path would be, how many moments of despair it contained—how reluctantly I would have taken my first step. But thank God for my faith in life's meaning, and for the growing sense of ownership for each and every moment, for claiming my life and letting it penetrate me with all its mysteries! For I find that I can have no question of my willingness to suffer because I am always washed ashore in new realms of growth and consciousness. What a miracle to lie open, to invite my life to hand me any lesson because I KNOW it will always be all right. To be able to invite pain to join in my experience and not to have to control my life to avoid pain is such a freedom!

We walk innocently into our griefs, and they carry us wherever we have to go in order to learn, to find meaning, to reach some kind of peaceful acceptance. We cannot control them; we ride them like a runaway horse. Our job is to stay on until the horse calms down and we are allowed to walk a while, to retake the reins.

- What do you need to let go of, that you are hanging on to?

- What does your hanging on provide you?

- What would letting go provide you?

- What celebrations are connected to this grief?

If you have trouble allowing yourself to grieve, deliberate use of memories may help you connect to your emotions. Certain songs can flood your mind with feelings, the glimpse of a stranger can remind you of a lost or dead friend. You don't need not be afraid of these responses. These flashes serve to remind you of the long journey you have travelled.

May 1988

My brother and I drove on an errand out to his office, down the highway five miles from where we both live now. Across from the industrial park is the dead end lane where we both grew up. This used to be the edge of town, the line where houses met farm fields. That line is further out now, I'm not even sure where. After our deliveries, I pulled onto Oak View Lane, to find the old house. The city has paved this little road. Even the driveways are asphalt now. The house is painted pastel, updated, more crowded since all the lots were built. I used to pasture a horse in the backyard, but the woods are only a line of trees to divide the lane from a subdivision of townhomes and the swamp has been drained.

Sitting here a moment, in front of the most tangible remaining evidence that once I was a child, I am reminded most deeply that the past does not exist. Even the shells of memory change. The streets widen or shrink, things change proportion, are added on or demolished. What I have to remember as I cruise the neighborhood is that my mind has done the same kind of rehabilitation: altered stories, enlarged or shrunk various incidences to fit a grander scheme. Things that I had forgotten by the end of the week when I was ten, have now acquired mythic proportion; and things that were arranged with hopes I would never forget, I have thoroughly forgotten.

Of course, I am doing the same thing with the present: weighing thought and events, shading them in my mind. What will be remembered and how, from this time in my life? Is there any pattern to this: is it pain or joy I most likely discard? Is it things that don't fit?

Fitting is important. We are all making up our lives. We are trying to be consistent with some interior image of who we are, where we came from, the possibilities for where we might go. Maybe what I need to discard even more thoroughly is the desire to fit in the imagery of my life. Let go the myth I have made of the past. Let go the myth I am making of the present. Then the way is open, horizon to horizon.

DEVELOPING FAITH

In the journey of the journal, we reach a point where we wear out the emotional bases for understanding ourselves. We reach a point where our capacity for change, our ability to cope with problems, our determination to plunge toward new insight, seem exhausted and we fear we have reached the end of the road. It is the nature of exploration, introspection, concentration, and honesty in the journal, to uncover at last this sense of limitation. We are confronted with the need for a new dimension. There are many questions that are not answerable within the vocabulary of search we have been using. At this point the journey confronts us with a choice of terminating it or allowing it to transform. How we respond to the proffered openness of a wider journey is a crisis point in the journal. And the crisis raises new questioning:

- Do you believe in "a way through"?

- Do you view life as a journey with some kind of meaning?

- What is the basis for self-acceptance?

- What role does forgiveness play in healing?

- What do you use as the basis for decisions made about life directions, relationships, career goals, psychological change?

- What force motivates your explorations?

- Is there a dialogue between the self and something larger?

- How have you gotten here? And how do you move on?

At this point, where we mourn the limitations to which psychology has brought us, we may find our understanding of psychology transformed. The unconscious mind into which we have dipped for revelation is the natural and accessible source of the next dimension. *The mind is the meeting point between psyche and spirit, the point at which the emotional quest becomes a visionary quest.*

Psychology, which is the study of who we are, connects us to our personal mystery. That is the exploration the journal of self awareness takes us on: becoming acquainted with the self in an interactive relationship of insight, healing and responsibility. *Spirituality, which is the study of Who Else and What Else is present, connects us to the mystery.* This is the exploration which awaits us, and which has been increasingly commingled in the explorations of self-awareness.

We are writers in a context, and given the social context of the journey in our culture, it is only natural that the visionary quest often speaks to us first in a psychological vocabulary. Psychology is the frontier of visions. In psychology we find the transformation and blending of the conscious and unconscious languages, the mortal and immortal voices. Psychology speaks of "whole-ness," and theology speaks of "holiness." Psychology speaks of "responsibility," and theology speaks of "atonement." Psychology speaks of "respect for the self," theology speaks of "respect for God." The shift in vocabulary is significant because it moves us down the spectrum of perception and shifts our context. We begin to see the world in larger terms than as a wounding ground and healing field for the self. We see life in its cosmic overcoat, and as soon as we do, we find ourselves in relationship to a Spiritual Other.

January 1990
Sitting in Sebastian Joe's after church, having coffee

and a muffin and time to write. Sometimes I need to take my writing out of the house so my life isn't crowding so much around me. This place isn't exactly contemplative, but it's the kind of background I have learned to tune out through years of journal writing wherever I find myself.

It's Epiphany Sunday, the day the Magi find the baby Jesus. I think of their journey and the T.S. Eliot poem which R. used in the homily this morning. It begins: "A cold coming we had of it, just the worst time of year for a journey, and such a long journey . . ."

This is exactly where I am: having a hard coming that feels like a mixture of birth and death, in the middle of a long journey. I am standing at a gate, stalled, waiting, frustrated, anxious, praying. I don't even know what I am praying for. That the way will open? That I will be ready when the way opens? That I will have the courage to step through? Or is it possible the gate is already open and only my unreadiness makes me perceive it as a barrier.

ME: Gate, will you open?

GATE: I am always open.

ME: What do I need to do to prepare myself to step through?

GATE: Be still. Know God.

ME: I do know God.

GATE: Yes, occasionally. Mostly you know your ego, these days. You know your anxiety. You know your misperceptions of what is going on.

ME: What is going on?

GATE: You are being given preparatory time. Time to prepare for the tasks which await you. You are being sustained well enough to use

         this time to prepare, but your preparation
         is turned aside, thwarted by your anxiety.
ME: I can't see the future.
GATE: You aren't ready to see it. It's right in front
         of you, like the gate is in front of you.
ME: I want to be ready.
GATE: Let go of your anxiety. Believe. Stop trying
         to manage life. Stop trying to create a safety
         net. I am the safety net. I am the gate into
         everything you long for.
ME: What?
GATE: Your soul.

Gary Zukav, in his book *The Seat of the Soul* (Simon & Schuster, 1989), speaks of our need to change our perception of the world and the self as a switch from a five-sensory human to a multisensory human.

We are evolving from five-sensory humans into multisensory humans. Our five senses, together, form a single sensory system that is designed to perceive physical reality. The perceptions of a multisensory human extend to the larger dynamical systems of which our physical reality is a part.

What Zukav means, I think, is that the five-sensory person can become aware of our nature beyond the self, beyond psychology. First, the five-sensory self must experience the empowerment of its own healing. The ego, which has been tattered by experience, needs to be stitched whole, and we need to know that we are capable of such healing, that we are, in fact, in charge of it. Psychology's great promise is that we can be free of the past, if we are willing to review what we came to believe as a result of our experiences, to reconcile with them, and go on. This is exactly the work we have been doing in the journal for self-awareness. This healing, the strength emerging in the ego, or five-sensory self, also brings us to the point of limitation: the point where we can go no further without leaping into the void, into an expanded view of the journey and the self. Later, Zukav says:

> From the perception of the five-sensory human, we are alone in a universe that is physical. From the perception of the multisensory human, we are never alone, and the Universe is alive, conscious, intelligent and compassionate. From the perception of the five-sensory human, the physical world is an unaccountable given in which we unaccountably find ourselves, and we strive to dominate it so that we can survive. From the perception of the multisensory human, the physical world is a learning environment that is created jointly by the souls that share it and everything that occurs within it serves their learning.

A writing student once said to me, "Psychology can fix all your stuff, but it can't fix IT." The "it" that remains, is how the self will fit into the spiritual dimensions of life; how we will each leap from being five-sensory humans to being multisensory humans, for this is the evolution demanded of us by the times in which we live. A restored ego-self is secure enough to let spirit surface naturally out of the inner journey, to perceive yourself, your life, your circumstances, and your life purpose differently. You will find you have been doing this anyway; a quickening occurs, and another layer of conversation weaves its way onto the page.

I don't mean you necessarily "get religion." What we

are aiming for is a moment of transforming enthrallment, a moment when the self of the journal meets the soul beyond the journal. It is the moment when we recognize that all along the journey of the self has been the journey to the soul. We have been journeying after ourselves and discover that the journey to the self is the journey that leads us into the universe. We come upon our own mysticism.

According to Evelyn Underhill's definition in her book, *Practical Mysticism* (Ariel Press, 1914),

> Mysticism is the art of union with Reality. The mystic is a person who has attained that union in greater or less degree; or who aims at and believes in such attainment.

Self-awareness leads to mysticism, because the work we have been doing in the journal cleans our perceptions so that we are ready to see reality, to see clearly beyond the self into a compassionate, intelligent, jointly created universe.

February 1990

It's early Sunday morning, been awake since 5:00 A.M., got up with this quiet dawn to write. Such deep forces seem at shift in me. I feel mountainous, volcanic, simultaneously very grounded, rooted, as a mountain must feel and also very fluid, open, alive, the way lava must feel.

I have stepped outside my ego. I think this means I have gone through the gate that has been haunting me for months. I still cope with ego, can be flattered, tempted, confused, etcetera but "I" am not ego. I am something else. I watch everything, track the convolutions of my thoughts, seeing how my mind works, not particularly caught up in its process. I do not know where I am exactly, but I know where I am not. I feel lifted up and set down in exactly the same spot in my life and everything is new, and everything is all right. I am blown open to the universe in a new way. This realization is not just a moment alone in the woods when nature grabs me out of myself, but a sustained awareness running through the middle of busy days. I am in new territory, and at the same time, I feel at home.

The need to acknowledge change began this journey, became the motif of the journal, and now frames our ongoing awareness. Change is the constant and we are constantly in change. To cease trembling before this awareness, to absorb it in our perceptions from the first entrance into the journal's pages, is the great gift that awaits our faith. We stand at the point of termination and allow our journey and ourselves to be transformed, to open to the questions which await us beyond self awareness. Even though we may not have known this was where we were headed, it is the most private and important work the journal will ever accomplish. It is "home."

> We shall not cease from exploration
> And the end of all our exploring
> Will be to arrive where we started
> And know the place for the first time.
>
> T.S. ELIOT, *The Four Quartets*

How to Start your Own Journal Group

There are several basics to journal writing in a group.

Create a group in which you and others will be comfortable writing with the option of sharing what you write.

Make a list of friends or acquaintances, a group from church, or other social connections, ask who among them keeps a journal or would like to keep a journal.

- Once you have a group committed to an introductory meeting, set a time and gather.

- You will need to decide several things fairly quickly: frequency, convenient times and days, length of meetings, and the mix of writing, talking, and reading time.

- Are you going to meet in each other's homes? a restaurant? a library or church meeting room? the YWCA?

Even more essential than where you meet, is that all members of the group have a similar sense of safety and confidentiality. I usually make the following group guidelines.

- People need to take care of their privacy first, and never write to be critiqued, or feel pressured to read.

- Confidentiality applies: whatever is shared in the circle, stays in the circle. If you want to talk about your own entry or story with others, fine, but you don't talk about any one else's entry or story.

- That this is **not** a therapy group. Others will listen, but not give advice or try to solve a person's problem based on what they read or share.

- If someone has an emotion, pass the tissues, but don't interfere. No one ever died from crying.

Decide how you're going to start, perhaps working through this book, topic by topic, with people writing between meetings on both the topic and their own usual mix of entries.

- Flow writing is always a nice way to settle the group, and for each member to discover what's on his or her mind.

- Use a timer so people can relax into the writing process, knowing they have ten, twenty, or thirty minutes to have their private thoughts and jot them down.

- No talking until the time is up. If someone finishes

early they can read quietly, go make tea, or whatever, but leave the writing space silent.

- For new journal writers, it often works best to start out with several shorter periods of writing, and gradually increase the time.

- You may want to use a talking period to ask for voluntary sharing of journal entries, to discuss books about journal writing, or read some of the excellent published anthologies or published diaries and journals.

- When someone reads, the only thing they really need is your attention, to be listened to, and for the group to simply say "Thank you," pause a minute in appreciation, and then move on.

Set a time, maybe three months, or six months, for reassessing the process. Go through regular reassessment, so that people know there will be a graceful way to make suggestions, leave, join, etc.

- Who wants to stay with the group?
- Who is ready to move on?
- How is the group process working?
- Have you got a good blend of writing and talking time?
- What new ideas have come to any of you now that you've had some practice?
- Do you want to invite in new members, or teach other interested people how to start their own group?

The most intimate, group bonding activity you will do together is write in silence. Trusting each other to create a space where collectively you respect this very private, individual process is a special gift that is not happening anywhere else in your lives. Honor the writing. Honor the silence. Honor your life stories and you will be fine.

About the Author

Since the mid-1970s, Christina Baldwin has been a leader of the renaissance in personal writing. The first edition of this book is a national classic, and was recently followed up with the publication of *Life's Companion, Journal Writing as a Spiritual Quest*. Her seminars have helped thousands of people become journal writers.

Baldwin holds a bachelor's degree in English from Macalester College, St. Paul, and master's degree in psychology from Columbia Pacific University, San Rafael, California. She lives in Golden Valley, a suburb of Minneapolis.

Christina Baldwin's workshops offer a communal experience in writing, working, and playing with life transitions. Her primary goal, in both writing and teaching, is to empower readers and participants, and to encourage people to apply their power toward social and spiritual change.

If you would like to book Christina Baldwin in your community or receive a schedule of upcoming appearances, contact Keane and Communicators, 3252 Lyndale Ave. So. Minneapolis, Minnesota 55408; (612) 823-4424. To be put on her mailing list and to place orders for journal tapes of meditations, workshops and lectures, write to: P.O. Box 27533 Minneapolis, MN 55427.